Praise for David Antin

"Ever since he began publishing in the mid-sixties, David Antin has been a remarkably interesting and intelligent poet."

—Gilbert Sorrentino, *New York Times Book Review*

"Antin's 'talk pieces' . . . belong somewhere among a standup comedian's rap, a storyteller's fable and a formal lecture."

—Michael Davidson, *New York Times*

"The wedding of mind and heart, of emotion and reality, which is tone: this is the triumph of an artist like David Antin; a triumph which contravenes its author's stated purpose."

—Donald Phelps, *Vort*

Other books by David Antin

definitions

autobiography

Code of Flag Behavior

Meditations

After the War (A Long Novel with Few Words)

talking at the boundaries

Dialogue

who's listening out there

Poemes Parles

tuning

Selected Poems 1963-1973

what it means to be avant-garde

TALKING

David Antin

Introduction by Marjorie Perloff
Afterword by the author

Dalkey Archive Press

Originally published by Kulchur Foundation, 1972

First Dalkey Archive edition, 2001

Library of Congress Cataloging-in-Publication Data:

Antin, David. 1932-
    Talking / by David Antin ; introduction by Marjorie Perloff ; afterword by David
Antin.— 1st Dalkey Archive ed.
      p. cm.
    ISBN 1-56478-271-9 (alk. paper)
    I. Title.

PS3551.N75 T33 2001
811'.54—dc21

2001028046

Partially funded by grants from the Lannan Foundation, the National Endowment for the Arts,
a federal agency, and the Illinois Arts Council, a state agency.

Dalkey Archive Press
www.dalkeyarchive.com

Printed on permanent/durable acid-free paper and bound in the United States of America.

to ely
for everything

if someone came up and started talking
a poem at you how would you know it
was a poem?

CONTENTS

Introduction

> Each of the sentences I write is trying to say the whole thing, i.e.,
> the same thing over and over again; it is as though they were all
> simply views of one object seen from different angles.
>
> —Wittgenstein, *Culture and Value*

In the Antin canon, which now ranges from the spare lineated riddle poems of the early sixties through decades of talk pieces, art essays, literary reviews, audiotapes, films, and even a foray into skywriting, to the forthcoming *Conversation*, a dialogue with Antin's younger alterego Charles Bernstein, *Talking* marks what is probably the key transition in the poet's career: it takes us from a set of Wittgensteinian exercises on meaning-making and its vagaries ("The November Exercises"), still in the mode of the earlier *Meditations,* to the first of the "talk poems," "Talking at Pomona," the text that sets the stage for the talk pieces which were to make Antin famous as well as controversial. Mainstream critics were quick to pronounce these pieces "*not* poetry" (and hence evidently dismissable?) even as, in avant-garde circles from Florida to France, Bucharest to Buffalo, new audiences were responding to these "not-poetry" works with delight and awe.

Indeed, rereading *Talking* in 2001, the main thing that strikes me is how avant-garde a book this is. I know that *avant-garde* is now a suspect term, that we have to surmount the barrage of commentary, whether on the Left or the Right, that tells us there *is* no avant-garde (if there ever was one!), that as Antin puts it so wittily in "what it means to be avant-garde" (published as the title piece of his third volume of talk pieces in 1993), there is only "the consolatory sense of the increasing belatedness and progressively more   attenuated virtues of each successive generation of poets   from blake and wordsworth to the present." This is, of course, a reference to Harold Bloom's theory of the "anxiety of influence," which Antin characterizes as an "inverted" idea of the avant-garde as

> a notion of first comers whose
> achievements were new and blocked the way to further
> achievements along the same path   an idea of patented
> inventions   each one acting as a roadblock   and the
> tradition as a series of bitterly fought retreats till the last
> "strong" poet finds himself like kafkas rodent or a beckett
> character backed into the last corner of the room

"maybe i'm such a poor avant-gardist," Antin responds, to this and similar decline-and-fall arguments like Richard Schechner's, "because i'm mainly   concerned with the present   which if i can find it might let me know what to do   and as for the future   it will find us all by itself." And he goes on, as is his practice, to tell a seemingly irrelevant story about his mother, unhappy in a California retirement facility, and his Uncle Irving, who wants her to come to Florida and "live the life of Reilly" with him, only to be hit by a car and killed, unbeknownst to the poet, soon after having made this offer. It is a story that brings home to us with a vengeance the Wittgensteinian precept that "Everything we see could always be otherwise." Being avant-garde, Antin suggests comically (and also sadly) means knowing how to deal in the present with a future one cannot imagine, much less anticipate.

It is this concern for the future latent in the present that makes *Talking,* now thirty years old, look so avant-garde today. For even as the early seventies bred moral parables about the Vietnam War and Nixon era as well as earnest, didactic antiwar poetry—works most of which now seem quite dated—Antin's *Talking* tracks the process of actually living through the war years in what was the beginning of the poet's own self-imposed exile years in Southern California. Perhaps the distance of viewing the discourses of war and the art world from his new family outpost in the town of Solana Beach, CA., helped Antin invent the improvisatory forms of *Talking* that, in various guises, have become familiar to readers of journals featuring "experimental" writing.

Take "The November Exercises," which Antin himself calls in the Afterword "a kind of a cross between calisthenics and spiritual exercises," using as found text the daily papers as well as a handbook for foreigners called *Essential Idioms of English.* Here is the opening of the first entry for Sunday, November 1:

(10:35 PM)   A pair of herons look at each other. Their pupils do not move and impregnation takes place. A male cicada emits a buzzing sound in the air above and the female responds from the air below. Impregnation takes place. Ravens hatch their young. Fishes drop their milt. Small waisted wasps metamorphose. There are footprints on the ground. Did shoes make them?

(11:15 PM)   Last month they laid off several thousand men.
The sound of their voices gradually died out.

(11.21 PM)   A star came by and asked some person, who will remain nameless, what should be done to make world government. The nameless person said, "Go away, you're a provincial!"

The combination of precision (the exact time of writing) and absurdity of these mini-narratives—part Zen koan, part tall tale, part grammar-book exercise—was to make its way into the Language poetry of the eighties and nineties. But Antin's are unique in their surprising variations. In the extract above, for example, the mode is not anything as simple as Dada non sequitur. The account of the impregnation habits of birds, insects, and fish is perfectly sober description, and the supposition that footprints on the ground were made by shoes makes good sense—so good, in fact, that one wonders why it deserves mention. But the second unit is quite different. The layoff of several thousand men would be registered by the pain of the individuals concerned, not by the sound of their voices dying out as perceived by others, although, strictly speaking, the emptied factory yard could conceivably be the scene of such a dying fall. As for the third item, the joke is on the narrator who imagines—we might say, provincially—that a "star" (star what?) has expertise on "world government." And besides, lofty ideals always become the source of someone else's derision ("Go away, you're a provincial!")

Antin, as he reminds us in the dialogue with Bernstein, was a child of the Depression. But his way of dealing with the world as he found it, has been, above all else, Wittgensteinian. In a recent essay on Wittgenstein for *Modernism / Modernity,* Antin remarks

> All of *Philosophical Investigations* can be said to consist of a *thinking-while-writing* that was in all likelihood based on Wittgenstein's own *thinking-while-talking.* For whatever else Wittgenstein may have been, he was an improvising, talking philosopher, whether he was talking to colleagues and friends in colloquia, or to students in lectures, or to himself while he was writing. His lectures were legendary. . . . His commitment to improvisation was absolute and quite self-conscious. He told [Norman] Malcolm that "once he had tried to lecture from notes . . . but was disgusted with the result; the thoughts that came out were 'stale,' or, as he put it to another friend, the words looked like 'corpses' when he began to read them."

Here is the key to Antin's own method, which makes its first appearance in *Talking.* In both "in place of a lecture: three musics for two voices" and "The London March," he experiments with controlled improvisation, recorded directly on tape, using both his own voice and that of his wife Elly (the conceptual artist Eleanor Antin). In "three musics," the occasion is provided by a "scientific" experimental design text about a farmer who claims to use a carved whalebone as an instrument to detect the presence of underground water. Within a few pages, this sober narrative, *read* by Elly, gives way to a series of practical questions on the part of the unnamed inlocutor (David in his *speaking* voice) as well as a third set (Elly again, but this time in her *speaking* voice) that questions those

iv

questions. The story cannot, it seems, be "told" in any straightforward manner, the questions, which is to say the noise in the information channel, soon overwhelming all linear communication. The act of telling the tale transforms it in a very wittily rendered piece of "thinking-while-talking."

"The London March" uses improvisation for more serious purposes. Set up as a radio play, with Elly "playing solitaire for various whimsical wishes," it conveys a terrible sense of anxiety on the part of a husband and wife used to being at the center of things (in this case, the anti-war activity in downtown New York in the late sixties), who are now thousands of miles away in a little beach town where, for all anyone would know, the world is perfectly peaceful and pleasant. Their baby son Blaise is asleep in the next room. From the periphery (here emblematized by the not quite organized London demonstrators to whom both David and Elly refer), they try to talk *about* the war and Washington politics, only to find themselves reminiscing about their college friends, lovers, early days of courtship—all the things that bring to life their former selves. It is necessary to do this, the improvisation implies, in order to try to make sense of the present. And even then, it doesn't quite work.

When more conventional lyric poets and their readers accuse Antin of being unemotional, I wonder if they have read "The London March," which is surely one of the most painful poems written in these years—a kind of slapstick version of Coleridge's "Frost at Midnight," where the talkers try to cheer themselves up by remembering what childrens' books were their respective favorites or whether Natasha was in love with Charlie or Letch. Again, this is a process work in which the thinking-while-talking becomes meaningful only in the course of the slowly evolving narrative.

In this context, the first talk poem, "Talking at Pomona" is not so much a departure as a Wittgensteinian improvisation that, this time, develops Wittgensteinian language theory as well. The word "theory" must be qualified: like Wittgenstein, who scoffed at all metalanguage, insisting that "Ordinary language is all right," Antin, as he tells Bernstein, has "a thorough distrust of the uses of expert language." "The vernacular," as he puts it, "is pretty permeable and admits new technical vocabulary when you really need it." But if "theory"—or more properly philosophy—is understood as "the pursuit of fundamental questions," says Antin, "I do the best I can at this in the vernacular."

The theoretical issue in "Talking at Pomona" is what "art making" means in the late twentieth century and why anyone should value it. This "subject which probably doesn't have a name," as Antin announces at the beginning of the poem, can't be approached by putting forward a series of generalizations or abstractions. Rather, the poet's improvisation—his thinking-while-talking, which is later revised and adjusted for the print medium of the book—can only proceed by circling round and round the topic. What is a painting anyway? Is it a painting of something and why do we need it? Why does a particular person like a particular painting? What do "painting relators" (art critics, connoisseurs, dealers, and so forth) do when they relate paintings to one another and relate to others about paintings? What is sculpture and are sculpture relators the same as painting relators? And how do these relate to those who buy these objects?

The very posing of these fundamental questions is, of course, a form of defamiliarization. In the course of his meditation, Antin exposes such contemporary truisms as the popular sixties axiom that "sculpture articulates space." "sculpture relators are interested in relations in   real space in three-dimensional space and painting relators are involved in   in non-real space whatever they are involved in is involved on a surface that is imagined to be separated from the space you walk into." Now suppose a given painting is placed in a doorway and "you smash the painting in half and go through." Is that, then, also the articulation of space and, if so, how does sculpture differ from painting? And the piece continues, pressing hard on such issues. In the course of "Talking at Pomona," everything we ever knew or thought we knew about the "art object" is called into question. Whose painting is it? The owner's (as in the Bob Rhinestone anecdote that comes up about halfway through) or the dealer's or the painter's? What is the painting worth? Can we quantify and say "brush strokes fifteen hundred   color"? And what does it mean to say that Cézanne was "intoxicated with what sunlight seems to do to volume"? "In the late painting by cezanne," Antin observes, "theres no mass no sense of mass because by the time he got through rendering volume and luminosity he has no room for mass   that is   the characteristic that he has to sacrifice."

In considering, one by one, the meaning of such words as "cube" and "slab," Antin adapts the Wittgensteinian language game so as to show how silly most of what was said about minimalist and conceptual art in 1970 really was. Not because he has anything against the artworks in question—works by Douglas Huebler and Dennis Oppenheim and Vito Acconci. Rather, he wants the audience to question their most basic assumptions and recognize the fallacy of this or that current fashionable art theory. For, as he comes to discover in the course of the talk, "human space is experiential space," space that can't be treated to abstract theorems about "art is...." In the end, as in Wittgenstein's *Investigations,* we cannot say what the "value" of a given artwork *is,* but we can delimit its parameters and say what it isn't. "it is possible," the piece concludes, "to construct make our art out of something more meaningful than the arbitrary rules of knot making   out of the character of human experience in our world."

When the Antins played the tape of "Talking at Pomona" on the drive home from Pomona, Elly, as David tells it, declared without a moment's hesitation, "that's a poem." What makes it a poem? To read the piece a second time is to note its status as a highly structured set of permutations on a few terms, in the vein of Gertrude Stein's permutations in *The Making of Americans* or *A Long Gay Book.* Words like "painting" or "sculpture" or "art" and their analogues and subsets are repeated again and again with a slight shift in context that makes them resonate. Like Wittgenstein, who once declared that "one can only do philosophy as a form of poetry," Antin is a *literalist* poet—a poet of denotation. He is not, that is to say, interested in shades of meaning or the subtle connotations of words, much less in their metaphoric or allegoric resonance. Nor is he interested in linear rhythm and the regulated chiming of rhyme or consonance. Rather his is poetry at the structural and syntactic level, with the syntactic units, as I have suggested elsewhere, rendered visually on the page with great intricacy.

And this brings me to the larger question of the book. Critics, myself included, have paid insufficient attention to Antin's bookmaking practice. Just as phrases and clauses are structured in the individual talk poem, so the book is, for him, always a woven verbal texture, a planned structure. In *Talking,* narrative, which will become much more central to his practice in *talking at the boundaries* and *tuning,* is not yet fully operative. Rather, the four pieces are united by their concern for serial definition. And here the cover of the book comes in. In the original, the inside and outside covers were a series of contact prints in which the standard glass-faced newspaper dispensers, placed in front of the local supermarket or post office, bank or branch library in the small beach town of Southern California, are viewed in the everyday surroundings. For what fascinates Antin is the contrast between the headlines, with their stories of disaster in Europe or Asia or Africa, and the setting of the newspaper dispensers on bland suburban streets, where men in shorts happen to be walking by or cars happen to be idling at the curb. It's all very idyllic—or is it?

The photo grid Antin made for the front and back, outside and inside covers of *Talking* thus gives us a visual equivalent to the discrepancies that are the thread running through the "November Exercises," the two improvisatory dialogues in the book's center, and "Talking at Pomona." *Talking* is not a collection of poems, not a volume from which to extract a putative *Selected* or *Collected*. Conceived and designed as a *book,* it prefigures such works as Joan Retallack's *Afterimages,* Steve McCaffery's *Theory of Sediment,* or Charles Bernstein's *With Strings*. An anomaly thirty years ago when it was first published, *Talking* makes perfect sense in the art/poetry book world of 2001.

And that's what it means to be avant-garde.

MARJORIE PERLOFF

2001

THE NOVEMBER EXERCISES

Sunday, November 1

(10:35 PM)   A pair of herons look at each other. Their pupils do not move and impregnation takes place. A male cicada emits a buzzing sound in the air above and the female responds from the air below. Impregnation takes place. Ravens hatch their young. Fishes drop their milt. Small waisted wasps metamorphose. There are footprints on the ground. Did shoes make them?

(11:15 PM)   Last month they laid off several thousand men.
The sound of their voices gradually died out.

(11:21 PM)   A star came by and asked some person, who will remain nameless, what should be done to make world government. The nameless person said, "Go away, you're a provincial!"

(11:29 PM)   Yung Kiang went rambling to the East borne along by a gentle breeze and ran into Hung Mung, who was likewise rambling around slapping himself on the ass and hopping around like a great bird. "What are you up to, Venerable One?" Yung Kiang asked. Hung Mung went on hopping up and down and slapping his ass. "Digging the scene. Digging the scene."

Monday, November 2

(12:15 PM)   She kept her head and he lost his. She telephoned the fire department and he drove up over the curb into a tree. Otherwise the whole house might have burnt down.

(12:17 PM)   When the rain lets up the drug will wear off.

(12:20 PM)   When you blow up a building you make it smaller.

Tuesday, November 3

(1:15 PM)   The architect designed the building in such a way that in the lower half each successive floor was larger than the one below, so that the floor of the higher storey provided a roof that shaded the lower storey, which had walls of glass, from the sunlight, although the lower floors were all protected from the sunlight by a grove of eucalyptus trees surrounding the building. In the higher half each successive storey was smaller than the one below, so that the glass walls were completely unsheltered by the floor above it. This was unfortunate because the eucalyptus trees reached precisely to the midline of the building. Since the lower storeys were shaded by the concrete roof above and the upper storeys were unprotected by the eucalyptus trees, they had them all cut down.

(3:15 PM)   In this code each letter stands for a complex number and when all the words are counted the sum will be in the plane of real numbers.

Thursday, November 5

(2:17 PM)   He wastes a lot of time and has a sense of humor. He looks out upon the park, resembles a driver, slows down, tastes fresh, telephones his friends, is invited to attend. If the bread dries out he goes more slowly, is as large as the park, gets nervous, loses moisture, fools around, is promoted, stops, borrows from him, comes out of the oven, is deceived, faces the park.

Friday, November 6

(11:17 AM)   Instead of beating about the bush he came to an end at 10 o'clock.

(10:23 PM)   During the past twenty years with what different countries has the United States broken off diplomatic relations! Why do they lay off workers in some industries just to take on someone else later? Why do most automobile manufacturers try to bring out new models of their cars each year? What do you do when the heels of your shoes become worn down? What is the difference between wearing down and wearing away? What do you mean when you say something has worn out? What do you do when the soles of your shoes are worn through?

(10:32 PM)   He said "The fish come out and play among the waters. That is the enjoyment of fish." The other said "You aren't a fish. How do you know what constitutes the enjoyment of fish?" He said "You aren't me. How do you know I don't know what constitutes the enjoyment of fish?" "I am not you and I don't know you very well. But I know you are not a fish and therefore you can't know what constitutes the enjoyment of fish."

Sunday, November 8

(10:00 AM)   To come across someone is to marry him. To give someone a ring is to argue with him. To stand for something is to pay for it. To drop someone a line is to throw him a rope. To take pains is to hurt yourself and be content.

To look up to someone is to be short. To look down on someone is to overlook him. If a watch keeps good time it stops often. When a plane takes off it leaves the ground. If you take off on Tuesday you will arrive on Wednesday. What do the stripes in the American flag stand for? Blood. What do the stars stand for? War. If you come across someone try and come with him again.

(7:30 PM)   While driving to Boston we got lost and drove many miles out of the way. Four men took part in the holdup. They robbed the owner of everything. The shipment of merchandise was delayed because of the railway strike. Traffic on the bridge was halted for several hours. He ran away from home when he was a child. They got married in Boston. We are going to the pier to see a friend. You will set the curtains on fire.

(9:00 PM)   Next day he came and settled down. But before he had settled himself he ran away. I said "Run after him" but you said "No, there was an end of him. He is lost, you will not find him. I confronted him with pure vacancy and an easy indifference. He didn't know what I meant to represent. Now he thought it was the idea of exhausted strength and now that of an onward flow. Therefore he ran away."

Monday, November 9

(1:30 PM)   I ran across several interesting facts about Mexico.
                 If it doesn't make sense it isn't logical.
              Why Mexican diplomats all drive in Mercedes Benzes.
                 If it isn't logical it may still be funny.
              The President of Mexico gets a commission.
                 It makes sense.

Tuesday, November 10

(7:00 AM)   To hear about it is to cause it to happen. It grows in strength you underestimate it talk about it increase it. You will get a good bargain enjoy describing it. It will happen and you will leave early. Before the accident on the corner.

It is doing well and you arrive on time. You are going to be musical and persevere by giving a seat to your friend. He diminishes gradually in the distance.

What happened on the corner increases in intensity. You can't resist being cheated. It has just started to happen and it won't ever get stuck.

(6:25 PM)   If you can't make something you can't enjoy it. Vests are dying out or doing well. The Roxy diminishes in the distance behind the 2nd World War. Hitler disappears completely. Uruguay has discovered Doctor Mengele and stood up for its friend.

(8:35 PM)   Cheer up and blow away. Everybody who visits me begins to leave permanently, which makes me happier to sit with him.

Wednesday, November 11 (Veterans' Day)

(11:15 AM)   I cannot keep up with you. We break in old and worn. "Have you got a cigarette?" means to count the days. Look at your watch. Someone is turned down. His hat is becoming to you. If someone breaks into your home he is a little large, new and stiff. Turn off the radio, stop talking, maintain the same speed.

(6:03 PM)   If I have got to leave early I want to leave early. If someone tells you to shut up count the days. He is old and worn. He leaves a message for you "I cannot keep my promise." It will soon be sent to you. It is accepted. Look at the clock and know what time it is. Did you obtain a cigarette? Turn off the radio? Stop talking? I cannot support you. Maintain the same speed as you. I must leave early.

(10:32 PM)   They tore down the old building and built a new one. In order to build the highway they had to tear down a whole block of buildings. The rope was too long so we cut off about two feet of it. If we cannot find an apartment we will continue living here. We have bad luck but we always make the best of it.

(10:43 PM)   If something is in his way there is only enough for a few. If a building is being put up someone displays his ability or his possessions ostentatiously. He is eating out, getting rich, showing off. He is going on vacation and putting on weight. If I remove a part of something by tearing it I cannot tell you from your brother, speak to you alone, tell you any secrets, distinguish between you day in and day out. If someone is in my way he is blocking my path unless there is enough of something to go around.

(10:57 PM)   "Hold still. How can I take your picture if you don't hold still. Hold still for a moment while I fix your tie." She went up to him and shook his hand as though she had known him for years whereas she simply knew him by sight. "Is there something the matter with Helen? She looks pale." "There is nothing the matter, nothing wrong. The mechanic says there is nothing the matter, nothing to fix."

21

Thursday, November 12

(11:05 PM)   Take care of him, call on him, follow him everywhere. Have the desire to do it, feel well, feel foolish. You will have some communication from him. If you laugh at him or ridicule him he will lose his way and get what he wishes. Anticipate it. If a prediction turns out to be true it turns out to be foolish. Eat a lot, laugh and joke with him several times. Make him the victim of my jokes. He will anticipate it in a final and definite manner in the hope of pleasing you.

(11:17 PM)   A thing is called by its name through the constant application of its name to it. How is this so? It's so because it's so. How is it not so? It's not so because it's not so. Everything has an inherent character and a proper capability. There is nothing which doesn't have these. A stalk of corn, an I-beam, a deformed man and Marilyn Monroe. Things great and insecure, crafty and strange. Frank O'Hara said that nobody could be his friend who wasn't Marilyn Monroe's friend. Was Marilyn Monroe Frank O'Hara's friend?

Friday, November 13

(10:17 AM)   Happiness is lighter than a feather and no one can sustain it. Calamity is heavier than the earth and no one can outrun it. If a building burns to the ground what do you do with the light bulbs? Do you take it for granted that it was old fashioned? Does it stand to reason to believe that the climate of Cuba will be warmer than the climate of Florida? In what country did an epidemic last break out?

(10:25 AM)   The riots were suppressed by the police, who were interested in sculpture as a hobby. The whiskey never appeared and he was revived by the sound of the radio. He keeps his counsel and remains home every night until midnight. What does it mean that the refrigerator smells of onions? That the cake tastes of ammonia? This music is beginning to make me nervous.

Saturday, November 14

(1:15 PM)   They stay at home every night. The sound of the radio suppresses the riots. If a place burns down it burns rapidly. A ship, a fuse and a curtain stand to reason as things taken for granted. As to that it is difficult to understand how they can increase in size unless they break out upon investigation.

(1:23 PM)   If I say that it stands to reason it means it is difficult to understand, that an epidemic has broken out, that we permit it to increase in size, which happened suddenly. We generally object to it, look it over, accept it without investigation because, in addition to that, we liked it. It made good.

Sunday, November 15

(10:11 AM)   Giants and fairies inspire the troops. They broke down the door and entered the room. Nobody thinks this makes sense, to believe in such things. Two teams have already dropped out. If you are ever in the neighborhood drop in and continue to feel despondent. The wind blew down the fence. The roof was blown off the house. I'm afraid the wind may blow the tent away.

(10:21 AM)   If after a quarrel two people make up someone bursts out laughing. It serves you right to meet someone half way. You may get away with it if you use cosmetics, unless something is too shiny. To laugh constantly unless you enjoy it, aches. I mean even if you had a good time, received good service and deserved it you can stick out your tongue.

(11:37 AM)   He has been punched, beaten, knocked unconscious. It doesn't make sense to try to cheer him up. You may sit with him but it doesn't make him feel happier. He is often absent when you criticize him. Then he leaves permanently and you run across him. He is executed.

Monday, November 16

(1:05 PM)   If you see about it you may never hear about it unless it disappears completely. Then it begins to grow in strength because you undermine it and unless you enjoy it you can't describe it. It happens early, before you begin earning a lot of money. Even if you get a good bargain you won't be able to stick to it and are finally cheated. It is doing well. You may as well stay at home, it's just starting.

(1:15 PM)   Hold on a minute, Germany took everyone by surprise or did most people expect it? After you've made a declaration a war can always be named after it. The President's death took everyone by surprise yet no one was surprised at their resignation. A former one, who was his friend, wanted to hold on and why would he have been better off in a hospital? Rich or poor, one has to prepare a report that remains in effect although you have put it away.

(7:25 PM)   In the scene above birds are flying, geese are swimming and chanticleer is clapping his wings and crowing in pride. Of course this only gives a true description of the scene supposing apprentices. A description must consist of measurements.

Tuesday, November 17

(11:53 AM) Between the aging overweight plane and the sleek jet we see none cutting a swath through the tops of the trees. "Our problem is money" the member said. "We've always wanted something we couldn't get."

(12:25 PM) The agents have not returned. Violence is taught in America in an off hand humorous way impugning character. Whoever chooses to do so is free and may regret it in a personal way, either directly or by innuendo.

Thursday, November 19

(12:53 PM)   They are extinguished and gaining force though we've been traveling at a very good speed. It's due to your carelessness that they assemble. You've erected several buildings in that place which will take hours to tear down.

(1:17 PM)   Upside down doesn't mean inside out.

Saturday, November 21

(1:25 AM)   In Canada there's plenty of snow. In Canada there are many lakes. Here is her raincoat. Here are her rubbers. There's no space for the box. There are four windows in the room. There's only one apple on the table. There are others in the bag. Here's my paper. Here are my answers. There's not enough bread for toast. There are no eggs in the refrigerator. Here are two nickels on the sofa. Here's a fine situation.

Sunday, November 22

(12:00 noon)   "Let's fuck here in the sun" suggested Carrie. "Why not screw here under
the bushes?" asked Paul. "Yes" replied Carl "be sure it's in the shade."
"Where did you put my sunglasses?" asked Carrie. "They're underneath
you" said Paul. "Me for the shade," decided Becky. "Yesterday I fucked
too long in the sun."

Monday, November 23

(12:13 PM)   "Excuse the radio" some of my companions complain with loud shrieks.
              When they came into town they thought there was going to be a banquet
              but after a short period they sat down under the clock and cut open two
              apples with a knife.

(2:37 PM)   His brother is talking English. One man is an Armenian and the other is a
              Greek. The waters of the Mediterranean are very blue.

(2:47 PM)   This country uses about 110 lbs of salt every year for every person in it
              but other countries use a lot of salt too. Farmers put out rock salt for their
              animals, wild animals hunt out salt licks, I gargle my throat with salt any
              morning that I remember to. If you've been poisoned and you swallow salt
              you can vomit. If you figure out that a pound package of Diamond Crystal
              Salt costs twenty-nine cents, a man who is worth his salt is worth $31.90.

(5:23 PM)   The waters in a surge brought out a bountiful harvest. None had the
              strength to climb out.

Tuesday, November 24

(1:25 PM) They each took hold of one end of the table and looked into the past. It was a matter of record. No one seemed to know how the building caught fire. There was a large sign outside the door that said DANGER. Who could keep track of all our expenses? The long distance phone calls we make every month? Why do they have that sign near the factory? What other materials do they have to dispose of?

(1:38 PM) "Sit still, don't panic," her father said. But people got up from their seats. My mother jumped up. The kids were alone when the building shook and the plaster fell. "There was a great blue flash over that way. I think the chemical company just blew up."

(1:46 PM) Ate too many apples. Threw rocks at a wasps' nest. Picked some pretty leaves that turned out to be a type of ivy. Were careless about falling asleep. Slept out of doors without enough of a good reason. Borrowed something from the owner of a leaky tent. Met someone I was trying to avoid.

(1:49 PM) Sometimes instead of asking questions you answer people—how to split and polish a thunder-egg agate, how to make a helicopter that will fly, how to make up for television. Questions are always coming into my mind. The purpose of a partial explanation or a vague or confusing one is to gain information.

        Example: If he holds up one hand for several minutes
                       the blood in his hand will drain downward.
                       When you come back into the room you can see
                       at once which hand is whiter.

(2:23 PM) They did not see this but if they had seen it would it have saved them? No accident has yet occurred but if it ever should would anyone be saved? How can a man bring himself heartlessly to ignore all appeals? I have always expected to and thought it only fair. If it would rain tomorrow I would stay at home. I determined that I would and finally succeeded. No one was able to state the case correctly.

(5:17 PM)   They have had men killed and expect considerable concern. They will never see this. I always expected to. I determined that I would. I thought it only fair. No accident has happened yet but if one does nobody will be saved.

Wednesday, November 25

(1:08 PM)   How does a friendship begin? You are introduced to someone, you talk, you meet again, you call each other on the telephone. Getting acquainted is not always easy. Just being introduced often gives some of us a bad time. Keeping talk alive after an introduction may be difficult. Sometimes when we've got a conversation going we make a remark so tactless that the talk stops dead. Even on the telephone we sometimes make the kind of mistake that comes back to haunt us.

(1:23 PM)   He knows the answer. She doesn't live here anymore. The potatoes seem to be cooked. Thunderstorms usually occur in the winter. The doorbell works all the time. Grass grows in the shade. It makes no difference. Burnt toast tastes good. She needs the music. They don't know the answer. Oak trees would grow very fast it seems near lunchtime. He believes the skies seem very clear. My watch seems to keep good time.

(1:27 PM)   A boy with marbles in his pocket has aroused the fire trucks. The fuses seem defective.

(1:32 PM)   A view of the mountains. Ice on the locomotive. Tapes for this recorder. Insects on the rosebush. Nails in the door. The propellers. A weird music. The actual trains pulling into the station. A light in the window means somebody is at home.

Friday, November 27

(12:32 PM)   Before the automobile has noticed it's carrying a beginner it's out on the
                 roadway. The instruction book gives a false impression of a real picture.
                 Everything you expected to handle with patient acceptance is now speeded
                 up and scattered. Relax, hold onto the steering wheel and pretend that
                 you're driving.

in place of a lecture: 3 musics for 2 voices

voice 1: *eleanor antin*
voice 2: david antin
voice 3: eleanor antin

this is the score of a controlled improvisation
that was directly recorded on tape
the spacings indicate the pace of the
performance but because of the limited com-
pressibility of type and the much less limited
compressibility of speech the notation is
suggestive rather than literal—the tape
recorded version of the work was performed
at St. Mark's in the Bouwerie.

A farmer from nearby Whidbey Island visited the psychological laboratory of the University

of Washington. He had with him a carved whalebone and claimed that in his hands the bone was

an extremely powerful instrument capable of detecting the existence of even small quan-

tities of water. To support his claim he said that several of his neighbors on Whidbey had

tried unsuccessfully to bring in water wells. Finally they had called upon him for help. He

had taken his whalebone grasped one fork in each hand and walked slowly over the ground. Sud-

denly the point or apex of the bone had dipped sharply toward the ground. When his neighbors

had drilled wells at the points he had located in this fashion they had found water.
What was

The farmer added that he was unable to explain his particular

the farmer's name?

Farmer Brown.

power. His neighbors were unable to use the whalebone in locating water. It had to be in his

hands before it would dip sharply indicating the presence of water. He was somewhat disturbed

by his ability and he thought that perhaps the university psychologists would be interested

in examining him and telling him why it was that he was able to use the bone so effectively

while others could not. He himself thought it had something to do with "magnetism" that

emanated from his body.

Why did he go to a psychologist? If he thought it was magnetism?

why didn't he go to a physicist or some other natural scientist?

Maybe he thought it was

But if he thought it was magnetism why would he think of
some kind of spiritual sickness.

sickness?   Then why not a doctor?
   Well maybe he thought it was some peculiarity of his body.

Anyway, he would be willing to demonstrate his ability so that the psychologists could see

for themselves. Perhaps then they could explain it to him.

I'm still not sure I understand

At this point in his story the farmer took a paper
why he went to a psychologist.
                    But he did.

cup and filled it with water and placed the cup on the floor.

Apparently even his neighbors

How do you know they waited
were disturbed. Otherwise why did they wait so long to call on him?

so long?   Also, where did the whalebone come
          It says "Finally they had called upon him ..."

from? It was clearly a divining rod "a carved whalebone." It was supposed to find water. Did

it belong to the farmer or to one of his neighbors who was unable to use it? If it belonged

to a neighbor, how did the farmer ever discover his gift? If it belonged to the farmer, why did

At this point in the story the farmer
his neighbors bother to try using it themselves?

took a paper cup and filled it with water and placed the cup on the floor. He then grasped

the whalebone and held it stiffly in front of him as he moved slowly about the room. When

40

the apex of the bone passed over the cup of water his arms trembled slightly and the bone dipped

toward the ground. The farmer showed signs of strain and remarked that the force was so power-

ful he was almost unable to keep the bone in his grip.

I wonder how close it had to be? How

precisely he could locate the water. Supposing it was very precise and led him to a water

cooler. If there was no other source available what if it led him to a water pipe?

The farmer showed signs of strain

Would it lead him to ice?

Or steam?

Do you think it would lead him to any reservoir of water? It

Or ice cream?

couldnt, because it would lead him to too many things. It would lead him to leaves. The water content of leaves is very high. It would lead him to cucumbers.

Maybe

The farmer showed signs of strain and remarked
Trembling?
the farmer was tired of trembling?

that the force was so powerful he was almost unable to keep the bone in his grip.

The psychologist thanked the farmer for his demonstration and said that he would

like to test the farmer's ability to locate water under controlled conditions, but that

this would require some preparation. Would the farmer be agreeable to returning for

these tests next week. The farmer agreed and promised to return at an appointed time.

Now it is obvious that the "evidence" the farmer cited as to his ability is not the kind

of evidence that would be satisfactory to a trained scientist.

The farmer wasn't citing

evidence. He wanted to find out why he had the ability to discover water and nobody else

did. He was disturbed by his peculiarity. He wasnt at all disturbed about whether or not

What evidence will be satisfactory. How shall

he could in fact discover water.   To whom?

the claim of the farmer be investigated?   *Let*

I wasn't aware that he was making a claim. He had a problem.

us see how the psychologist designed an experiment which would yield data bearing

The psychologist had a problem.

upon the problem.
But they were not the same problem.

When the farmer

returned to the psychological laboratory the next week he was greeted by the psycholo-

gist and taken to one of the laboratory rooms. Spread around the floor of the room

were 10 pieces of plywood about 1 foot by 1 foot in size. Numbers from 1 to 10 had

been marked upon the top of each square. The pieces of plywood were resting on tin

cans about No. 2 in size. The psychologist explained that he had used a table of random

numbers and had picked 5 cans to be filled with water while the remaining 5 were left empty.

What was the farmer's name?

Farmer Brown.

No, what I'm curious about is why the farmer didn't receive a name.

The psychologist

But they named the island.   Whidbey Island.

didn't receive a name either   A lot of times.

One.   Two.   Twice, they named the Island   and the university.

It was Whidbey Island and Washington University and was the department of

psychology and it was a psychologist   Well, why

a psychological laboratory. They didnt

didn't they name the psychologist.

I dont know.

They even describe the whalebone

They didn't name the people at all.

with great particularity.   It was

He doesn't describe the people at all.

a carved whalebone with an apex and two forks   that is to say   two branches

coming to a fork   and the farmer had owned it   and the farmer had no name.

No.

And he also had no physical characteristics either.   He wasn't tall, he wasn't

But he trembled.

short, he wasn't fat, he wasn't skinny.   But he trembled. I was thinking

We're aware that he trembled and he was   and he was upset   and

that.   and he was upset

the psychologist greeted the farmer   he had neighbors   and

        he also had neighbors   he did have neighbors

were the neighbors upset?   They were

      Well, they waited a long time before coming to him.

reluctant to call on him?   The neighbors were reluctant

     Yeah, so they were something.

to call on him but came to him at last. He trembled. He was upset. They were probably

somewhat disturbed. The psychologist wasn't troubled. He merely greeted the farmer.

It said he greeted the farmer.   Did he welcome him back to the laboratory

     Right.

when he came back?

     He was greeted and then   He returned to the

laboratory. He was greeted and then taken to one of the rooms.

What do you think the psychologist said   when

he greeted him?   "Hello, Farmer Brown?"

"How do you do, Farmer Brown?"   "Come this way, Farmer Brown?"
                                                    "I hope you're all

                    "We're ready for you, Farmer Brown."
set Farmer Brown, hee, hee, hee."

Perhaps the farmer was not named Farmer Brown. He said "I'm ready for you, Abraham."

          And then Abraham said "I am ready."   "I am ready doctor"

          The doctor said, "Come this way Abraham." And Abraham

followed him out.   Abraham was wearing a buckskin suit. No, probably not. He

was wearing overalls
  he was wearing overalls   He may have gotten dressed up better to

see the psychologist. Well he may have expected an experiment of some sort so

                                  No,
maybe he was just wearing overalls everyday clothes but he could have worn Sunday

I imagine the farmer was wearing his Sunday suit
clothes.   But since he didnt confess to a priest

I doubt if he was religious
        That's right, so what did he have a Sunday suit for? for wed-

      A Sunday suit is for driving into town
dings or funerals.   going....   going into town. Farmers go into

                That's true. Maybe it was for going to
town in their regular overalls I've seen them.

the firemen's annual dinner.   the fire department's auxiliary
                    Right or going to the university perhaps he got dressed up

You think he regularly visited the University?
                                        No but perhaps he did this time. So maybe he put on

                    Well it was the suit that he probably wore when he went out.   Now the
his good suit

question of what the psychologist was wearing is a curious point. Was the psychologist wearing

a suit also?
              By the way I would expect that he would wear his regular work clothes when

when he came in   because he always did it and he used the whalebone in his regular work-

clothes. So i dont know what he did the first time he came but   no, he also did the experiment then he had to show him i suspect he came both times in his regular work clothes   because

he was probably getting very superstitious about the whole thing   and maybe he thought the

the magnetism   He wanted to come as he always came when he dealt with it.

So Abraham

arrived in his workclothes   the psychologist was dressed in a suit   probably withoι

the jacket and with the tie open   with the tie loose and the shirt open at the top
                              Right.   open

button.   Maybe his sleeves rolled up because he had just placed
          Maybe his sleeves rolled up.

plywood over cans   and the knees of his suit
                        Well he could have given orders   he didnt have to do

        and the knees of his suit.... if i know psychological laboratories he had done it
it.

himself.   **Probably not.**   **Probably there**

    There was nobody to do it for him?   There's no other people so....

was no money to be spent on using assistants for this experiment so that the psychologist's knees

were still dirty from crawling around on the floor placing plywood over tin cans

                                                        you dont think

                Probably not overly clean.   **Psychological laboratories are not swept**

the floor was clean?

with that immense regularity.   **That's right.**

        Well this was one of the rooms.   This could have been a smal

                  Which would have meant it might have been dusty

room that wasn't frequently used.   Mmm.

    Well there would be no reason to have it overly clean considering the farmer

And the psychologist was wearing a sharkskin suit

worked out in the earth anyway

without the jacket   unless it was the summertime   in which case he was probably

wearing a tropical suit without the jacket.   Tan. A tan tropical
                                                    What color tropical suit?

suit and a white-on-white transparent shirt   with short sleeves so he didnt have the

sleeves rolled up.   and probably a tie pin.   But then
              That's right.   and pink freckly arms

he would have had   well perhaps freckled arms bare arms
                                                    and yellow hair.

receding yellow hair   and he had
                    i was thinking of yellow hair on his arms

receding yellow hair on his head   and steel rimmed glasses   unless he was a snappy psycho-

logist and wore shell rimmed glasses   and he looked like a Village Independent Democrat

which is also possible   unless he was a very handsome young man   which is also

possible   and he had very dark hair   with very blue eyes.   And he wor

a turtle neck sweater   Not in the summer. He wore a sweatshirt
                      Not in the summer he didnt.

and the farmer was somewhat irritated at him because the farmer was wearing a Sunday suit

and the psychologist was wearing a sweatshirt.

                        All right. Go on.

What did Abraham say?

Not Abraham.   God.

said that he had used a table of random numbers and had picked 5 cans

to be filled with water while the remaining 5 were left empty.

Winston.

Winston Horowitz.

Who's Winston?

Abraham.

is the doctor?   and who's the farmer?   No, Abraham? Just plain

He emphasized that under 5 of the sections of plywood were cans

Abraham.

Abraham?

of water

Eggers?   Abraham Eggers.   Abraham Eggers had reported to Winston

It's good.

Winston Horowitz

he emphasized that under 5 of the

sections of plywood were cans with water and under 5 others   *5 other sec-*
                                                                    Why could
                                                      Winston Horowitz

tions
'nt he be called Winston?   because he had Jewish parents? there's no reason not to
                                                                    No. I'm

he was called Winston   He even preceded the cigarettes. He
not anti-Semitic.

may have been named after Winston Churchill.   His mother and father remembered

that speech "on the beaches..."   "We will fight them on the beaches

"We will fight them in the cities ..."   "blood sweat and tears." And his parents had
Oh that.

with tears in their eyes remembered Franklin Delano Roosevelt and would have called him

Franklin Delano Roosevelt but they remembered the speech of Winston Churchill and they

named him Winston Horowitz.
                                                    Maybe because if his name was

Franklin he would have been called Frankie and they didnt like that name thinking it was

                                                                    Well they were
vulgar. But Winston   he would just be called Winston all the time   or Winnie

they probably had never heard Winnie and would have imagined Winston lent a certain dignity and probably would always have called upon the remembrance of Churchill be-

cause it was the only Winston they had ever heard.   Winston Delano
                                            Maybe he's Winston Delano

Horowitz?   That's quite possible   Winston Delano Horowitz   but nobody would

have known that   because he probably signed it Winston D. Horowitz   which he used to sign

all his checks. If his name was Winston Horowitz they assumed Winston would have reminded

everyone of Churchill   whereas it reminded everyone of the cigarette   That was not
                                                                    Later.

their fault. In those days they had Lucky Strikes which had given up its green.   Was it

Lucky Strike that had the green package   and the green metal case
                                                        They had Raleighs and

No they had a green metal case which they   there was in fact an ad that said
Chesterfield.   Philip Morris

"Lucky Strike goes to war"   which meant that Lucky Strike gave up its green because

the green was a metallic   involved a metallic color and they gave it up for the

war effort.   Yes, in fact when I was in Kansas last year Ted Berrigan
            Oh really?

and I picked up several of the old cans of Lucky Strike with the green paint on them

and then we remembered the slogan "Lucky Strike goes to war."

                                        And I think that they

had not known of the brands like Winston.   Yes I think he probably
      Then you see the psychologist as being very young.

was a young psychologist   Proba-
                    You see him as being something like 27

ably.   He might have been very old   but I doubt

it
     Probably every one else kept sending him lower and lower in the echelon and finally

                    They probably gave him to the youngest   snappiest young doctorate
he was sent here.

around.   One whose projects were not involved to such an
                                  .   Of course he had to

extent.   They had to have the time to even consider the subject.   They gave him to the
have the time.

free doctorate.   So it would have to be a younger man.

any of the Europeans would have sounded somewhat different anyway   it would have to have beer

an American psychologist   I've never heard of a European born behaviorist.

And there are older American behaviorists but I somehow see

him as a young 27, 28 year old psychologist named after Winston Churchill.
                                                              and the farmer?   And what about Abra-

          I see Abraham as being a middle-aged man.
ham?

                              I would think of Abraham as being

          about 50

                                                                    He emphasized
                    Why dont you go on?
                                              Yes.   But

Abraham   wasnt aware of his gift   I dont think   until fairly recently

He emphasized that under 5 of the
No.   Probably it was a late discovery.

sections of plywood were cans with water and under 5 other sections were dry

cans and that the arrangement of the empty and filled cans was purely a random

one. The psychologist now wanted the farmer to take his whalebone and attempt

to divide the 10 squares of plywood into 2 groups   one group would be the 5

covering the cans filled with water and the other group would be the 5 covering

the empty cans the farmer did not need to make his choice in any particular order he was merely to divide the set of 10 sections into 2 groups of 5 each.

Let us examine this experiment in some detail. We shall pay particular attention to the

kinds of choices the farmer might make the hypothesis which the experimenter is testing and the

manner in which the test of the hypothesis is to be made. The psychologist may reason in

this way, "Let us assume that the farmer does not possess any particular powers which enable

him to locate

Perhaps you should call the farmer Abraham and the psychologist Dr. Horowitz.

Dr. Horowitz may reason in this way "Let us assume that Abraham does
as you read.

not possess any particular powers which enable him to locate water with his whalebone that the only factor which is operating in determining his choice is chance."

This is the null hypothesis which the experiement is designed to test. The

possible outcomes of the experiment can be demonstrated in a simple way

by the rules for permutations and combinations. Permutations refer to the

number of arrangements (orders) in which a set of n distinct objects may be

arranged. In general the number of permutations of n distinct objects taken

r at a time is given by the equation $nPr = \dfrac{n!}{(n - r)}$ where n! is called

factorial n and represents (n) (n - 1) (n - 2) and so on or the product of all the successive integers from n to 1. In the problem at hand the number

of orders in which 5 sections of plywood may be selected from the available

10 is $10P5 = \dfrac{10!}{(10 - 5)!} = \dfrac{(10)(9)(8)(7)(6)(5)(4)(3)(2)(1)}{(5)(4)(3)(2)(1)} = (10)(9)(8)(7)(6) =$

= 30,240. This figure gives us every possible order i.e. any 1 of the 10 sections may

be selected first. This choice may be followed by any 1 of the remaining 9. This choice

may be followed by any 1 of the remaining 8 and so on until 5 have been selected but

in this experiment the psychologist is not going to demand that the farmer select the

set of 5 cans containing water in the particular order in which the psychologist put the water into them or in any other particular order. All that the

psychologist is interested in is the set of 5. Once the set has been selected as

far as he is concerned the set of 10 5 8 2 3 selected in that order is equivalent

to the set 8 3 2 10 and 5 selected in that order or in any other possible

order. It may be noted that the set of 5 selected objects or sections may

themselves be arranged in (5) (4) (3) (2) (1) = 120 orders according to formula

5. Thus dividing 30,240 by 120 orders we obtain 252 ways in which a set of 5 objects

may be selected from 10 if the arrangement is ignored. In general the number of combinations (arrangement ignored) of n distinct objects taken r at a time is given by

the equation $nCr = \dfrac{nPr}{rPr} = \dfrac{\frac{n!}{(n-r)!}}{r!} =$

$= \dfrac{n!}{r!\,(n-r)!}$ or in the present problem $10C5 = \dfrac{(10)(9)(8)(7)(6)(5)(4)(3)(2)(1)}{[(5)(4)(3)(2)(1)]\ [(5)(4)(3)(2)(1)]} =$

$= \dfrac{(10)(9)(8)(7)(6)}{(5)(4)(3)(2)(1)} = \dfrac{30{,}240}{120} = 252.$ Now the best that the farmer could

Abraham

possibly do ....   Now the best that Abraham could possibly

do in the present experiment would be to select the particular set of 5

which happened to be those with water in the cans and this particular selection

would be 1 out of 252 possibilities. If only chance factors were operating in determining the selection and this experiment was repeated an indefinitely

larger number of times, then we would expect this particular set to be selected

with a frequency approaching 1/252. Thus 1 divided by 252 gives a value

of .004 (more precisely .00397) and this may be regarded as a probability.

As pointed out earlier we shall regard probability as a statement concerning theoretical

relative frequency. We say that the value of P is .004 or that this result would be

expected by chance alone only about 4 times in 1000. This value of P is obviously smaller

than .05 which we agreed to regard as significant. We also agreed that a significant value of P would result in a rejection of the hypothesis being tested. Hence if Abraham is

able to choose this particular set of 5 with the aid of his whalebone then we should

undoubtedly feel that the probability of this occurring by chance alone is sufficiently

small that the hypothesis with its related assumptions is not considered tenable.

At this point we shall do well to consider what the rejection of the hypothesis

means. If the hypothesis is rejected this means only that the experimenter is not

willing to assume that chance determined the selection. It does not prove that the

whalebone has had any particular influence upon Abraham's choice. This is something *that the test of the hypothesis has nothing to do with. The psychologist might be*

willing to assume or infer that the whalebone played some part in Abraham's selec-

tion but he would undoubtedly do this only if other possible explanations had been

ruled out in terms of experimental controls. What are some of these alternative expla-

nations? Without the experimenter knowing about it Abraham may have used the toe of

his foot to tap the cans under the board. Since in this manner the cans filled with

water could easily be distinguished from the empty cans it would account for a perfect

selection upon Abraham's part. If this was the basis of Abraham's selection then obvi-

ously the whalebone had nothing to do with his choices. Abraham might even deny that he

had used this cue   the sound of the can when tapped with his foot   if questioned about

it. But the psychologist knows that many of our choices and judgments
Dr. Horowitz?

But Dr. Horowitz knows that many of our choices and judgments are based upon

factors of which we are not aware. It would be Dr. Horowitz's responsibility to have

ruled out by observation or by some other control this possibility.   *Again*

Dr. Horowitz would want to make sure that Abraham had not tapped the tip of the

whalebone on the tops of the plywood sections. If Abraham had done this his choice might be

71

determined by the differences in sound of the sections covering the water-filled cans and

the sections covering the empty cans. He could thus make a perfect selection of the

five water-filled cans and the experimenter would reject the hypothesis of chance. But note

again that the rejection of the hypothesis of chance does not establish the validity of

Abraham's claim concerning the influence of the whalebone.   Another possible ex-

planation of the perfect selection might be   that Dr. Horowitz had spilled some of the water

on the floor in filling the cans. This water might have been carefully mopped up but slight

cues may have remained   the absence of dust or the cleanliness of the floor under the sections *of plywood containing water   as a result of the mopping might provide cues for*

Abraham's choice. Or perhaps Dr. Horowitz gave some sign   a holding of his breath or an

unconscious biting of his lips as Abraham moved the whalebone over the sections

containing water. Abraham's choice might thus be based upon one of these unconscious

gestures or reactions of Dr. Horowitz   without of course Dr. Horowitz and perhaps even

Abraham being conscious of the fact that these cues were the basis of Abraham's choice.

Or

When will he ever get to the whalebone?

when will the whalebone get to him?

Look   supposing a man comes by   while Abraham is out in the field   with his

whalebone....   And he comes by   somehow in a helicopter   and he takes photo-

graphs of Abraham ....   and Abraham is bent over his whalebone and he takes photographs

from right above his head   and you see the top of Abraham's head and his back and it's

bent and you see his arms down   and he develops the photographs and there is no whale-

bone.
        He just looks like a hunchback.   What if

                                                                    What would that mean?
Abraham's lying?

That would mean that he never found water out in the field   but it would mean

that he'd have to be able to find it in the laboratory   or it wouldn't be worth his

while.   So that the question of lying
            Well, he'd be found out too quickly.

is not a question of his having no power   but his having power to find the water

            in a laboratory.   which is
                  Or   having power over psychologists.

power of finding water in a laboratory.   So Abraham specializes in psychology laborato-

ries.   And he's never found water in the field.   But he

has a whalebone.   And he comes in.   And he demonstrates his power with the whalebone over a paper cup.   And then he tells Dr. Horowitz, "I can find

water in the field, look."   And he's confident   that when Dr. Horowitz sets up

the experiment   somehow or other   he'll find water.

                Now Dr. Horowitz   suspects something of

this sort. Dr. Horowitz   has already   in examining the event   considered   that A-

braham   has forced him into errors of negligence   or errors of physical inadequa-

cy.
                That's right, that he can't hear him when he taps with his foot and that

That he can't see him lean over and tap the cans with the whale-
he can't hear him

bone.   Or finally   that Abraham has
                              that he's sloppy and leaves water

          that he's gotten him nervous enough   to be sloppy   and leave spots of
   all over the floor

water on the floor   or that Abraham   manages to elicit

from him   physical cues   involuntarily   that is   Goes pale.
                                        Holding his breath.

Dr. Horowitz   seems to be waiting for Abraham.   And Abraham...   And to expect that he was

that he was very susceptible to Abraham.   And Abraham   seems

77

to be waiting for Dr. Horowitz. He's looking for Dr. Horowitz and Dr. Horowitz is

looking for him.

How many times do you think he found it?

He must have found it or Dr. Horowitz

He didn't find it.

wouldn't have abandoned the null hypothesis.

Well he couldn't have

Why not?   Say he

done it more than 3 times.   He'd have gotten bored.

did it twice.   What do you mean?

Did what?   Well how many cans did he

Five.

On the first try or the second?

find?

What if he found 4?

They'd run the experiment again.

On the first try.

What if

They'd still have to run it again.

he found it on the second?

The results

Well what if he found 4 on both shots?

would have been inconclusive.

In a well designed experiment these

factors and many others that the experimentalist may suggest must be controlled if logical conclusions are to be drawn concerning the results of the experiment. It is

to be emphasized that these logical conclusions are derived from the structure of the

experiment and the nature of the controls exercised. They do not come from the test

of the statistical hypothesis. The statistical test indicates only the probability of

a particular set of results upon the basis of the statistical hypothesis tested, namely

that chance alone is determining the outcome. It does not prove that the farmer bases

his choice on the whalebone or that the whalebone is in any way influential in determi-

ning the outcome. If the experimenter rejects the hypothesis of chance he must still *examine the structure of his experiment and the nature of his experimental controls in*

making whatever explanation he does make as to why he obtained the particular results

he did. Needless to say most psychologists in terms of their knowledge of experiments

upon related problems would want to examine critically and carefully the experimental

controls in the face of perfect results upon the part of the farmer. The accumulated

evidence upon the effectiveness of divining rods in locating water is negative.

THE LONDON MARCH

mmm   hmmmm hmmm   hmm hmmm   yes   what shall we play for?
                              ready to play?

                                   i think thats enough   or is it too much?
i dont know

              mmm hmmm   hmm   hmmmm hmm
                                   what are we playing for?

                                        ah ah
how about Humphrey?   **hmm?**   **you want to play about**

              no!   yeah play for him to lose   play for him to
Humphrey?   **no   no   we were still**

              oh yeah   no   lets play for   you get a good
after his   **we figured he was going to get elected**

audience   lets play for   oh we're going to have a swinging party   the first game i
     yeah   **no we got a swinging**

83

played   thats stupid
party   dont you want to play for the Vice-President to be wiped out?

        because its not going to happen   so why should we waste a game?
                                                                        thats

        oh you want to play for a great crowd tomorrow?   in London?   100000 people?
true

                a half a million people   play for a half a million people in
250000 people   okay

London to protest the Vietnamese war tomorrow   their government'll be shocked
                                                okay   oh

                                oh no   i dont want our people to get massacred
it'll probably be a massacre   if there

                                with that many people they dont get massacred
are a lot of people well maybe they wont   is that

        if they stick together they wont
right?   usually   of course there were a lot of

about half a million   about ten thousand
people in Chicago too   half a million   a few thousand

didnt they   not half a million
                         okay lets play for a big turnout   i dont know what

        - nothing ever does any good   but lets put it this way
good it'll do   but

it cant do bad   if an action   people have to act   and if the action doesnt do

bad   thats something   nowadays   the way i would put it

                                                              oh i dont
                              come again on that i didnt get that

know   i was just talking

85

what else should we play for?   you want to play

yes

for that?   all right   we're playing for a crowd of a quarter of a million

half a million!   a half a million people to protest the Vietnamese war in
beings

London tomorrow   why we had half a million in New York
            thats implausible   i know

            yeah but this is their government   they're getting absolutely
but it was our war

furious   im sure   its a terrible government
            okay   that's true but they're furious

            all right let it sound like
at their government for different reasons   some of them

            let them make an extension
are furious at their government for taking any action against Rhodesia

the other ones are furious at them for not taking any action against Rhodesia

all right   you want a quarter of a million

people to show?   okay   course   you can multiply whatever
          yeah   it's more probable

they say here   by   about four
  if you said a half a million people youd have to get the Fascists for Mosley

out on the Vietnamese thing on your side   i dont think there are that many

        theyre not activists when you come for the big parade
activists in all of England

of the year or the big march of the year to Washington those people arent all ac-

tivists
  well if they sent out contradictory reasons for example if they would have

told the people   if they would have told the racists of England that the parade

was to remove all the negroes from England and you told the Mosley fascists that

the thing was to remove all liberals and   if you told the others   it was to put

an end to the war   youd probably get half a million people   all of them on the

all right now   we're playing for a quarter of a million people to come out
same street

to protest the Vietnamese war in London   tomorrow   Sunday afternoon
and intimidate the police

honey dont add to it   i said i want to play for that
okay   all right   so play

i have a right   im looking for
for it   okay   you want to cut   **okay you want to cut**

sugar   where?   it figures
        the sugar is over here   where the sugar always is

                                                        did you mix the cards
        theres more sugar in the cabinet   yeah

                                        remember to get more cards   we
ive been mixing them   for a long time   okay?

need new ones these are getting old and stupid already
                                        we wanted to get a chess

        well   for fifty cents we can get cards too
set   all right then you can give these

            he doesnt need them   he doesnt
to Blaisey   yes he does he likes to tear them up

tear cards he cant tear them   here come on
                    throws them away   he bends them

        all right next cards a couple of sixes   youre having trouble

89

huh?   i know   theyre no good anymore and
well theyre sticking together   theyre so old

this is wet here   this is from the tea   feel it
                         its not wet here   i know that but that hasnt got

                                                        oh good   thats the
anything to do with it the way theyre sticking to each other

first six   very good   i just saw an
                    it looks like were going to get a good crowd

ace
      were all playing for images huh?   why couldnt we

                                                      im not playing for
play for something reasonable?   like Hubert Humphrey's death

that right now   nine   all right now   a red five
                                           couldnt all the candidates

        all of them?   wouldnt that be great
die?   all of them should die of Asian flu   Hong Kong flu

im not talking about those flus God forbid   im very worried about it
strikes all of them   i know

                              its foolish isnt it?   people dont die anymore of
youre always worried   yeah

influenza do they?   well penicillin helps them doesnt it?
          not very commonly   i dont know i

            whats the   antibiotics help?
dont think so   well they may be of some use theyre

                              then why did people used to die of them
generally of use in secondary infections

and they dont anymore
              the reason people died of them very often was because of

secondary infections but sometimes they died of them because they hadnt built

up any immunities to them like the Asian flu of 1918 i think it was an Asian flu

                                                                but
of 1918 that really decimated   quite a few people

they dont happen anymore
                they havent happened in a long time and i guess it may

                                                        like pneumonia
very well be because of the ability to stop secondary infection

for instance
                yeah which developed very often   as a consequence and they can

                        thank god   red three
stop pneumonia   yeah they used to have this

        i dont want to hear it
joke   if you have a cold go home and get pneumonia and then we can

                mmm   ace of hearts
cure you   oh Jesus!

                                        ace of spades
lots of luck   come on!

jesus!   forget it

         yeah   looks like our boys are not going to be out there

     five of hearts   you arent calling for the right cards   i need a

      i said a red three   i forgot

red three   oh i didnt hear you theres a five of clubs

about that

     okay   this is for Harold Mcmillan

                  the ace of spades

to receive no peace   the ace of spades   wrong ace

                     nine?

bad scene   the ace of clubs?   ugh   this is pathetic   we're going

                     doesnt matter

to   this is a very bad scene   why do you want that one?

doesnt make any difference   you were right one move hurt it did exactly what it would have done trying to follow the logic of the other one

                              ace of clubs
                                      ace of clubs?

theres an ace right over there   i saw it   black queen
                                  where?   **an ace**

            we need that one   a red eight would be of some use
of hearts   **no it**

would help business   its the last card its hardly worth it we're not getting

much of a turnout in London   okay so far we're down to a crowd of about two

                                    two thousand? honey look thats not true
    thousand it looks that way

            look we're down seven it means we're shy seven thousand
half a million!   **all**

94

right 2500   anyway lets see what we do

these cards are worn out   from being requested to do

things for us   we need a new set thats not used to being a flunky

i could have so easily had a neurotic miserable
        a genii

life   no dont laugh at me   i
        used to be a 98 pound weakling

have all the things in me   that push comfortably in that direction
                                                        everybody has

oh   but i give into them   do you?
                                i dont know everybody knows how to

                how would you destroy yourself?
destroy himself sometimes   i dont

know   i could do a good job of messing around with it   what would you do?

what would i do?   i was wasting an awful lot of time wasnt i?

yeah but you always waste time you consider it not waste
                                                maybe   there are times

when you think that youre wasting time and youre not there are other times when

you think youre wasting time and you are i think that i was marking time for a few

                                                        you dont want
years actually   it seems to me   what would you say?

to leave me and blaisey do you?   you want to leave me?
                          no   uh uh i dont want

                          you dont want to leave me either? do you
to leave blaisey either   i dont want to

96

                                        no but why do you always put us in the same
leave you i dont want to leave blaisey

breath?
          im not im putting you after each other   i dont want to leave my 1953

chrysler imperial i dont want to leave solana beach right now i dont even want to

                                    we're on the west coast? this shitty
leave the west coast right now

place?
          its hard to imagine that this is california it doesnt feel like it   does it?

    it feels like we're on the north atlantic   its unbelievable   this is about

                                    and when its warm it still gets freezing
the fifth day in a row of cold fog lying over here

at night
          yeah   it freezes at night its freezing in the morning it gets beautifully

97

and its
warm during the day the change in temperature what is it its something like 25°

getting polluted
            well pollution is only during occasional periods its not always

                                    by the way i want you to know
it happens to have been today and i think they day before

that my nose hasnt cleared   will you do it before you go to bed tonight?
                                                        try salt

            its so easy to do you have nothing to lose honey   it might be easier
water?

for you to   you know im going to do it every day
                                    as long as it helps ill try it

                        all that phlegm coming out of your mouth its disgusting i
i cant stand waking up in the morning

didnt know there was so much there
                    well its the california weather   ive been waking

up every morning   with a stuffed head   it reminds me very much of the fall days in

easthampton   it really does   remember how the bed and everything else

in easthampton was always damp   the whole house   its not as bad   this house doesnt

                 no   yeah   but   there was something repulsive   there
feel quite as damp because you can air it out but

was something repulsive about it   yeah
           well   the other one had a sort of rotting quality   it was as if

                          yeah this one doesnt have that feeling
  the wood was secretly rotten behind a wall   yeah

   do you find this an uncomfortable house?   i dont
                          no its very open but its not un-

comfortable   though things do get wet   and you have to keep doors and windows yeah it really is   if

closed somewhat   otherwise everything gets kind of soggy

you live by the beach thats what happens

i was talking to this guy in cardiff while

we're saying that now were playing for a crowd

you were waiting for blaisey

of about a quarter of a million tomorrow to protest the vietnamese war

now that

no   what did the man

youve said it do i have to say it?   all right i understand you

say?   the cardiff man?   the cardiffian

he was the guy in the liquor store

which liquor store?

blaisey always used to wander in there   he's right next to the butcher

oh   i always think of that as a grocery store

well he has groceries too   but he's

oh i see so you were
basically a liquor store and   i buy the l.a. times from him

talking to him?   a young man
            yeah he's also going to palomar college.   on the g.i. bill

he owns the store?
                he's the kid who works there   he's not a kid i mean he's a veteran

and   he works there   and he was   explaining to me   how he used to live   not in

the desert   a dry area around rancho bernardo   and he says its very hot there   almost

as hot as in escondido   and he says when he gets down within two miles of the beach

                                                                            it gets
three miles really   when he drives down toward the shore it changes climate

cold huh?
        yeah   it gets damp and cold   he likes it over here he's now living in

cardiff   he goes to school out in palomar   and palomar is hot around san marcos

is the school hot?   no your
its really pretty hot out there   he says its pretty warm out there

school?   its not that far from the water
       its much warmer than here its   its a little bit in probably

just far enough in and its open to the sun for some reason or other it seems to be

always a bit warmer i dont know why   remember i told you i came back the other

day from there and as i was driving on the road i could see a wall of fog coming in

from the water side   i was coming on 5 and going north and i saw these drifting

clouds of stuff coming in coming up over the hills and you know the way five how long does this last?

runs through carmel canyon and there was this wall   it was like gas warfare

i dont know   i can imagine what gas warfare must have looked like you know when

you see a wall of clouds advancing   its a very strange look   you can really ima-

get me a black jack

gine it   okay come on

black jack

                theyre well mixed   i dont know whats going on here   red

        and a red five   ah shit

five   well you dont

                        is that the only other black king

have many things to put anywhere   i dont think

                                i cant even get a jack   its ridicu-

we're doing very well   i have a feeling this game

lous

black four   looks like nobody cares very much

                                        yeah but we need a black king
now youve got a place to put a king anyway   well

ace of hearts would be all right
                    thats no good   thats no good either

                    hmm

                                        ace of
          we've still got a chance   this is only the second game

hearts   would be of some use   theres a
                    yeah   could run to the four

five somewhere   a black five would be useful
          a jack would also be nice

okay   now   i dont think we're going to win this game

                                        i know not any
theres a black jack its not the greatest

more it isnt
      if i had that red ten i could have found a use for it and id

                               maybe you should have left
have been better off

the black jack   though it doesnt matter anymore
                  it doesnt matter   were very far

                i cant believe it
down   we're going to get a crowd of three   bertrand russell and his two

                      i forgot
friends   theyre going to protest the war   ralph whatshisname?   remember

    heres a ten
charlie?   remember armand's friend charlie   who worked at the school with

i never met him   dont
him he was married to a girl named natasha   charlie was a kind of sad loser

say that i hate calling somebody a loser its like theres some kind of a right way

to be a winner
      he thought of himself as a loser he was a kind of sweet   sensitive

                               so he
depressed guy   who later on was working as a secretary for bertrand russell

might of come out of it
        you'd think so at least his life should have been more

                      in england?
interesting   but we met him on the train and he was just as depressed as before

     he and that guy ralph were the two guys running that thing for russell

in england?   i never met him
    yeah yeah   and then he came back here and had a very bad

what did they do? harass him?   well
time   no i dont think so im not talking about that

theyre harassing that other guy
                              well they harassed the whole group and I suppose they

harassed him as much as anybody   but i didnt bring it up because of that   i meant

                                                        why?
to say he seemed to be a strange guy to be involved in that scene   he was so

pallid and the role seems so colorful   did i ever tell you about natasha his wife?

she was a dark french-israeli who was always trying to live up to her mediterranean

background being sexy all the time   she was trying to make everybody in sight to

                        was she?
prove how attractive she was   not especially she wasnt especially unattrac-

tive either   charlie thought she was terribly attractive   she was so dark and

french and jewish   and he was so white and blond and american   and she was always

making life difficult for him   because she had nothing else to do but be colorful

i think they had a child or two and he finally left her for someone who had five

more children and the last i heard he was supporting both women seven children

very protestant
and im not sure he was living with any of them   while working for

russell   paying alimony for all of them and working for the peace movement and probably

probably had to take a
should have been working for birth control at this point

job with the f.b.i. to survive
                    he used to work up at that barnard school that armand

                                                            how
worked for   barnard school for boys   then he got a job somewhere in chicago

would i have met him
                i thought you had met him once   he was an old friend of mine

i knew him before armand did   i met him when i was working at the translating outfit

the three of them charlie natasha and their friend letch i think he was living

with them too anyway he spent a lot of time with them at their depressed

apartment on christopher street   where charlie was supposed to be working on a

thesis on dylan thomas and letch was working on a thesis on the most depressed artist in the world nicolas de stael   and i was working on my bull play at the

you were pretty depressed too
time   natasha had nothing to do but be colorful and sexy

that kind of writing wasnt for you
i dont think i was so specially depressed   yeah

that kind of uptight writing is always
but i dont see what was so depressed   it was mistaken

depressed its always got a tight collar no matter how good it is   i remember

what it was like   you remember   those were the days i used to think i was an

actress   i wasnt bad at all   i just couldnt stand going out and
          yeah what an idea

looking for a job
            yeah and if you got one you wouldnt have been able to stand that

that happened too   it was just when i was beginning to get a few jobs that i
either

stopped wanting to be an actress
                        thats what i meant   being an actress was pretty

                its a horrible idea am i glad i never made it   i spent
deprived too   **you didnt want to make it**

all that time with madame daykarhanova   i dont want to talk
                        yeah because she hated you

about that   she wanted me to be an ingenue   thats the one thing i could never

have done   yeah but i couldnt make it   what they
            oh i dont know   you looked like one

were looking for was some kind of updated corliss archer   all those jews at

actors studio had a mad crush on southern accents and i never saw a magnolia tree besides i was never smooth   madame was right about one thing   did i ever tell

you what she said about me   she said if i was going to pick
                    yeah   you mean about

my nose id reach around my back to do it   well i never
                         she was probably right too

said i was smooth   bill hickey liked me   i never wanted to be
                    as joan of arc

an ingenue   if i say so myself i did a good joan
                              the whole idea of being an actress

you know   the kind of actress they were doing plays for is a deprived idea anyway

i only went into it because of that vision i told you i decided everything i did

was false so that the only thing left for me to do was become an actress i did it for consistency
                                                            and then

spend two years with a white russian creep expiating your sins   thats pretty

       the whole time was pretty deprived   it gives me the creeps to think about
deprived

it   but i finally got my chance to be a southern belle   at the Coliseum   to
                                          as a villain

raise money for the NAACP with ozzie davis   i thought my drawl was so lousy it

made me want to scratch but when it was over ozzie davis hugged me
                                        he probably

never saw a magnolia tree either

                            okay lets play the cards
                                      well

       im telling the cards now for the last game   we're playing now
tell them

that tomorrow   sunday   i dont know if thats now even   sunday
                                                        in any event   that ha-

                              in london there should be   about a quarter of a million
rold mcmillan regrets it

people protesting the vietnamese war

                    not bad
                              lets hope its not a slaughter   the sweet

british bobbies   the british bobbies to whom one can look up on the street when

                                                                        you know
one comes home   and see the club descending

you make such a funny face when you say something ironical   i adore you
                                                                        youre

              black four   youre funny   or a red eight and a
a sentimentalist

black seven   we better get an ace of diamonds or something
          take it   yeah   we better

get something   fast   otherwise there're going to be three people out there

                                        oh   those poor people come on
and theyre all going to be butchered   come on

jesus
          thats bad   we're really in trouble at this point   we're not doing well

              black seven
ill tell you   a black seven would be helpful but its not that helpful

considering we havent turned up anything of real value   go ahead

                                                        well i dont know
              if theyre depending on us we're through

what should we do?
                    we dont have any course   and we lost already   we didnt get a

well it wasnt a quarter of a million they have a hundred thou-

single one out there

sand

if three people come out maybe theyll realize its time to go home

okay   thats it

maybe charlies children   actually i think charlies children

are all in chicago   **i dont know   i thought for a while he did go back to**

there are a number of sweet gentle natured deprived types in the peace

england

movement   maybe theyre not deprived   he may not be that deprived

charlie was a strange guy

i met him   remember that childhood friend of mine you met when i was working

i wasnt with you then
for the translating outfit   that was filled with old communists

the owner was an old communist turned capitalist   the translators were all old

communists and the printer was a beautiful grey-haired leftist older woman from

new england she used to wear blue work shirts and no makeup   and she led a strike

against the communist owner for demoting gloria actually he promoted her   the

negro receptionist because she was so bitchy and turning all the customers away

jane called out everybody on strike   and my partner   the guy i used to edit the

russian automation journal with was afraid not to go out on strike too even though he hated gloria because his mother was the editor of the last stalinist journal in

america and he was afraid jane would tell on him if he crossed the picket

      i told you i wasnt going with you then
lines   i think i was going with millie   she

            i get depressed whenever i think of her
even got a job there as a sort of assistant editor

well mitchell was a kid i went to elementary school with   he was the only one

i knew who'd read the whole king arthur in malory and knew how it all turned out

      i used to love king arthur when i was a child   but robin hood was
  instead of the howard pyle version

my real hero
      bill wandered in one day and somehow i recognized him now he was a

physicist manqué out of princeton   natasha and charlie and letch were friends

of his   also manqué   from princeton   which seemed to specialize in deprivation

the fifties were depressed for everybody   remember the city college cafeteria

millie and dicky friedlander and gene kates   how could you ever go out with

millie   she was like a cloud   she was my
                i guess i was interested in meteorology

best friend from music and art but i never really liked her   i think i admired

her for being so close to insanity   it was like with roberta fox   i went to visit

her at the mental hospital   the nuns had given her some beads to say the rosary with and she got her meals and she didnt have to go out to look for a job   i think

i kind of envied her
                    sure   those were the days of carson mccullers and j.d. salinger

i think i felt sort of inferior because i wasnt crazy   i used to read all sorts

of books on schizophrenia   that girl with the needle   and kept looking in the

mirror for symptoms
                    millie wasnt really very crazy   but i dont suppose anybody is

in the end its probably nothing more   or less   than a way of being

stubborn   but it used to be very prestigious   look at allen "ive seen the

                                        but its still a lovely poem
greatest minds..." greatest minds   horseshit   sure

its a lovely poem but not because its honest whatever that means its because

well he's from the fifties too
of the way its full of shit   yeah but you forget

it   anyway mitchell came around with a new set of special characteristics

he was playing the cello then   he got together with nestor   who was head of shipping

a black guy who had an instrumental group   he used to sing   bill was doing

arrangements for him   managing for him   they were going to make it big on the

theyve got a great
porto rican radio stations *mi corazon* kind of thing

national style
                yeah its even better than ours   he liked the whole idea

i think   of a kind of depraved baroque   he took up with this girl   she was

the sluttiest broad you can imagine   but she was slutty on principle   it was

an image in her mind   she always managed to make any affair she had seem like

getting laid by six truck drivers in the back of a car and then she'd always tell

you about it or see that somebody else told you about it   bill got married to her

that fitted
                                 no it was a mistake   she never forgave him for it

i remember we went to visit them at their place   joanie and me and charlie and

natasha   and she went around the place showing us where there was a crack in the wall where she threw a dish at him because he kept on playing the cello or where

he hit her when he got jealous because he thought she was making it with the janitor

sounds very sexy
                    yeah   all this time she conducts the grand tour of their in-

                                            oh come on!
flamed passions he's playing bach on the cello   no life is very

poetic   its just that its lousy poetry   thats what charlie and natasha were

doing and letch   making poetry   im sure it was all part of the plot   for letch

to be "in love" with natasha for natasha to know it for charlie to know it   it must

have made them much happier in bed   they came over once to hear me read the play and i had to keep my eyes down all the time to avoid having natasha send me

you were just being mean you couldve been a gentleman and looked
signals too

interested
i suppose but they didnt hold it against me anyway and we all went over

i wish we had some now
to minetta's and ate zabaglione together   you're al-

werent you going with ruth at that time
ways hungry   yeah   that was later

she was a funny idea of passion too
after i left the translating company   i

suppose   she was probably like my play   it was an idea of cool style that you

were supposed to believe was a seething volcano underneath   the idea is that

124

thats a style i never had any use for
you read the style for being tense   i know

yeah i always wanted to be like anna magnani
you like more *sturm und drang*   then

i dont know
why do you complain when i say you look good with hair under your arms?

. always feel so messy   so i dont have the courage of my
                    thats part of the style

convictions call me a liar   or i got older   but i remember the time i decided

to seduce you   you were still going around with ruth   i figured that we'd been

friends all this time   you were the best friend i had   and the only reason we

hadnt made it together was because i thought you werent supposed to do that with a friend   that was my idea of passion   strangers in the night or something

someone gets off a motorcycle   i remember i put on my best dress and bought a

bottle of caviare   yeah and you threw me out
                    youre always thinking about eating

oh come on   i did not   you looked terrific and it was a great idea   but i was

still going around with ruth and there was all that unfinished business   you

know   being unhappy together we had to work it out   you know you have a certain

obligation to your passion   especially when its not doing well   that was one

of the times she committed suicide and painted the outside of her door with

126

she would!

iodine   i think she thought it looked like blood   whats the difference

                    yeah but some styles are better than

    everybody's entitled to his style

others

                                          that's it   its a wipeout

                    well   what should we play for now

                                                lets play

                                                      no no i

    for natasha to be married so that charlie doesnt have to pay her alimony

dont want to play for that   no i dont like to play for things like that

        you dont want to play for that?

you dont like to play for seriously minor things?   lets play for igal roudenko

                                  i dont think the cards like to be brought

and the progress of the peace movement

into politics of that nature   they really dont   they like to be brought into immedi-

ate important things   no no lets play
                    immediate and vicious and whimsical things

          for nixon to receive a transplant   for spiro agnew to be

hit by an oncoming taxi and nixon to be standing on the curb   to get a heart

attack   spiro's heart to be taken from the mangled remains and transplanted

into nixon   combining the two greatest virtues of our leaders   agnews heart and

                                                           no
nixons brains   you want to play for that?

you know what im going to play for?
                    mcnamara to publish his collected poems?

no im going to play for

lets play for mcnamara to publish his poems   so that i can review them

no   im going to play for

id like to review mcnamaras collected poems   in

im going to play that

caterpillar   what are you going to play for?

the world bank to go bankrupt?   what are you

ill play for you to become head of the art department   so you

playing for?

dont have to run the gallery   no

so that i should have to do lots of paper work?

you dont have to do paper work   what paul?   he doesnt

as head of an art department?

do paper work   he cant type

thats not paper work   thats clerical work   no you

know what i mean   pushing through things   you know paul actually has a seat on

the committee on committees   i didnt believe there was such a committee it sounds

you never have to show up
like a joke   oh you always do   thats the most important

thing about it   showing up   its one of the most powerful committees in the school

so you'd never show up   i dont
nobody knows what it does   harold urey is on it

like harold urey
          you dont know harold urey   he is a chemistry professor at large

honey i dont really want you to be head
thats what they call him "at large"

of the art department   i have nothing else to play for so im playing for you to become head of the art department

                    do you realize i just found out that linus pauling is

           does he teach?   yeah   linus pauling is a nice
on our staff   id like to meet him   id really like to

man   he's for peace
  meet him   but he's apparently called "in residence" which means he's

not in residence   i think thats what it means but id really like to meet pauling

yeah   he's a peace man   he hasnt said anything about the vietnamese war has he?

                                            but harold urey is
yes he has   he's said a number of things   but im curious about him

a reactionary facist beast   a tito-facist beast
                             tito-facist beast?   actually he

              yeah   but now he doesnt say anything i havent heard him say a
used to be a liberal

word
     thats because the liberals are worried about student rebellions now   all theyre

worried about are students   but he was one of the people who protested the

            well that was such an obvious farce
execution of the rosenbergs   not in those days

in those days   so he pats himself on the back and remembers
                        no now his big thing

is he wants to publish a list of punishments for students   he doesnt believe that

they should go in ignorance of the consequences of their actions   its going to be

very popular   what they would get if they did something   for example   for electri-

fying the professor-at-large's chair they might be electrocuted   no seriously   he would have given them all sorts of incredible ideas that they never had before   for

if he ever suggests anything like

infesting the cafeteria with cockroaches they would

that in the senate will you stand up and second it with a complete list of these

things they'd get punished for   and you should give a long thing with all these

great crimes and then you let them know   you let them know that what youre doing

is giving the students ideas   will you do that   you promise me?

why do i have to

dont put your hand down

promise you?   i always do silly things like that anyway

if munk doesnt call on you keep your hand up   and if he still doesnt call on you stand up and demand to be heard

he'll never want to call on me after the last time

thats another thing   what happens there?   munk only
i seconded a motion of his

calls on   you said once they didnt call
    no   they have to call on you   its like a club

on you   if you keep
        no they called on me   i insisted   i kept raising my hand

waving your hand they have to call on you?
                yeah   if youre a member of the senate you have

a right to speak   its a club ely   its like the senate   you have to speak   even

                        all right   we're playing that you
if they think youre a jerk   we senators

should become head of the art department here at ucsd when paul leaves
                                                        ah

i have nothing else

its a drag   i dont want to become head of the art department

to play for   im really not terribly intrigued with the idea

i really dont want to

then lets not play for it   what should we

be head of an art department

play for then?   oh "acting head!"

i could become "acting head" and then i'd never have to act

right   right   theyd have to raise your

then id be a kind of impersonator

salary anyway   wouldnt they?

they could make me king of the world and id prefer that

that would be the best   so far id never

they could make me intermedia chairman

heard of that

thats true   i could become the chairman of the department of inter-

not bad   we need

medial art

a red nine   wait   wait   wait   wait a minute   you see what happens
          a red nine

as soon as we play for something else?
                              yeah   it shows you   they only want me to

          become head of an intermedial art system   which are we playing for   that i

                              no   we're playing for acting head
was to become acting head of the art department?   i wonder if

                                                  intermedial jesus
theyd let me become head of the walking-on-the-water department?

                    come on baby   lets go

          i cant pull a card   every time i open it   its useless

wait a minute   there's something else here we're not paying attention to

a six of hearts here?   there was something too important about the

other thing for them to pay attention to it   eight
                                  a black five   eight

its not moving enough
                  i have a feeling we're locked in

we'll find that five   if you place
                        this one

the nine of clubs there   its pretty
                  that puts us back in the ball game

good   we made eleven   but im
        yeah   i dont really think so

sure there may be some way
                        no   there is no way   we dont have enough

well let me just see a second   is there an eight of

things to fiddle with

spades   actually you dont even have the cards out

we dont   we need too many

yeah theres no seven of hearts   no   theres no

all right so

we won this one   anyway   sort of   so far its favorable   lets see if its

going to be an overwhelming possibility   because if thats the case we'll have

they always like to play

found out what they like to play for and what they dont

for this kind of thing   even if they fail you

yeah   it turns out that scapular

whats a scapular divination?   huh?

divination is different   shoulder bone bets

138

why isnt that any good?

chinese divination   i said its different   it used to

be called on for very important things   these things can only be called on for very

trivial things   because we cant get any information about tomorrow in england

well we ought to be able to find out soon enough from the newspapers or the radio

we'll know what it means anyway   we'll be
yeah   soon enough   but not from england

able to figure out from what they say
                         at the present time its a quarter of ten   its a

quarter of ten here   all right   about six o'clock there   about time to call

when we wake up they'll be in the middle of it
up my mother   whatever it is   itll

be on   good luck

                    why should one feel more united with that than with the situation in

            i dont want to talk about that
biafra   at what point do you draw the limit

                all im sure of   those great african countries arent doing anything
of identity

they dont care
                i just want to know at what point do you choose to be concerned

i dont know at what point i choose to be concerned   they should probably yell

about that   those children are starving
                                but i hear   for the best political reasons

            i dont know what they should yell about but those children
right   some of my best friends

140

are explaining to me   the biafrans never had it so good   the nigerians were the suffering

yeah   its a white plot

ones   the children are catholic propaganda   no?   what about

when you say those things   how can i play for this dumb thing   everything

rhodesia?

i play for   its all inconsequential   theyre only interested in being petty

and mean   now im playing you should become head of the art department   acting

so that we

head of the art department   when paul leaves

so we can be invited to boring dinners

its not to be a social climber   its so that you dont have to find things difficult

and you can make a lot of money

so we can be invited to boring dinners and go

away bloated and indigestive

why dont we play for sabbaticals?   or

honey   im always for that   is there anything i wouldnt
guggenheims?

like more than a sabbatical?
we could take a guggenheim to england and we could

go out on the same demonstration   except   i hate crowds

i always hate crowds

i dont even care if theyre on my side

Talking at Pomona

what i would like to talk about   really   is a subject that probably doesnt have a name

if i were to give it a name it would sound kind of pretentious   and it might be

misleading   so   let me begin by reminiscing slightly   last quarter   we have a

trimester system that has quarters   it is an absurd system   i set about to ask myself

out loud   with a group of students   who were ostensibly concerned with art

what we could do to make a discourse situation in art   meaningful or comprehensible

now that sounds a little vague but what i really wanted to know was this   how can

you think about making art   and i use the word art as an undefined at the moment

how can you talk about it in such a way   that   it will lead to making more art

and the making of more art will itself be rewarding rather than a diminishing return

now how do you set about looking at art making   as something that will be

valuable to do   and the value of which will increase as you proceed to do more of it

im afraid this sounds like an absurd thing to say because people who normally come to a graduate school or to undergraduate school   to be art majors or graduate students

normally assume that it is valuable to make art   whatever that is   and typically

they have in mind the things that people have always done when they made art   and you

know there is a kind of consensus   a low level consensus   about what art making is

i mean without placing a utilitarian role upon what it does to you say   there is a kind

of function that people seem to attribute to it   nevertheless   they know what it is

beforehand   people think they want to make paintings   or they want to make sculpture

now this is a commonplace and obvious idea   of course very few people have any

clear idea of what it is that a painting ought to be that somebody should want to have it

for example   if any of you or all of you are graduate students or artists or whatever

or art makers   and i say to you   "you want to make paintings and youre really interested

in making furniture right? i mean you want something to hang on the wall   right over

the sofa and they have a persimmon colored sofa   and you want one that will give them

pleasure   so that they will buy it?"   and at that point you will either say "what is he

coming on?"   or you get up and start trying to get out the door   or show me the

door   you think thats a very offensive thing to say "what do you mean i make furniture what do you think i am an interior decorator?   no im not an interior decorator

im an artist!"   i said "well i thought you were an artist and you wanted to make paintings"

paintings   you know what paintings are in the art scene   theyre seven feet by

seven feet and the important thing to know is that a painting is big   it is very important to

know that a painting is large and not easily portable   a painting is a flat non-portable object

frequently covered with colors and usually stretched canvas over a support   and the important

thing is to realize that when people look at it automatically   in the beginning

uninitiated people walk into a place to see it   they dont think of it as a painting   i

said "oh   thats a painting?"   "no you dont understand painting is about...."   and

then theres a dead end   painting is about something   that is not easy   i

mean theres a kind of feeling   a great consensus that its not easy   its never easy

the one thing you know from painters who paint is that painting cant possibly be easy

they struggle about it because it would be easy if lets say the little lady   the proverbial and

mythical little lady who down in our area around san diego   we think of as the little

lady from la jolla the   little lady of la jolla has a gold frame painting and thats not what

you want to make   and she bought it in balboa park and you say "but whats the matter with buying a little painting in balboa park with a frame she hangs it there she looks at it often

it gives her pleasure"   and thats not what you want to make because what you want to

make means something else and i say "but that doesnt mean anything?" no what that means is

that that woman has a set of historical tastes that she loves and she is attached to her taste and

she wants to stick to those ideas that she knows very well   and   she will be satisfied

by it the way she will be satisfied by having a particular dish served to her once a week

by her cook   lets say her spanish speaking cook to whom she doesnt speak because she

doesnt speak spanish but this particularly peculiar dish that she expects regularly   her taco

dinner and   she knows what she wants in art it tastes a particular way   now my young

artist or old artist doesnt want to make that kind of art because hes not making food hes not

making a consumer item   so all right   youre not making a consumer item youre

making a painting   and its a big painting   and   what else is there in the painting

that is why are you carrying out this unnatural act say   with respect to a large piece

of canvas   stretched on a support   i mean what is this all about   i mean there

is this thing and its heavy its non-functional   it acquires dust and you put colors on it

and theres a sigh   a tremendous sigh   and they point to other paintings that is to say its like with other art   and it turns out after a while   that this art

this painting relates only to other paintings   that is to say it relates to other paintings

in the minds of the people who relate to other paintings   there are a set of people who are

painting relators   and these painting relators relate your painting to other paintings

which is how you know these are paintings   now in order to make a painting of the sort

that is related to other paintings by painting relators you have to find painting relators   thats

very important   painting relators are essential to artists   sometimes these painting

relators are other artists   and sometimes theyre people who do nothing else but relate

paintings   they have sometimes been thought of as critics   sometimes theyre hustlers

called dealers   and sometimes theyre people who   are just sort of wandering around

with nothing else to do but relate paintings   they sometimes relate sculpture   which

is about the same business   that is sculpture has a similiar career   i didnt pick painting

because i think of it as less or more than sculpture   that is in sculpture for example

there will be a man who will have a theory of sculpture and he will relate things that other

people will   for example   im giving a parallel example that is im not leading into greater

depth here what im assuming is that a man   publishes   an announcement in some accessible place saying that   he will pay a reward for the capture of this notoriously

non-dangerous criminal   who is among the twenty most or least wanted men by the united

states government   the name of the man who published this is douglas huebler   and he

offered a reward of a thousand dollars for the capture of this notoriously non-dangerous man

who the police also wanted and   he was going to pay a reward for the capture on the basis of

selling the documentation   that is to say he was going to sell the documentation involving

the apprehension of the criminal and his offer to pay the thousand dollars and when he did

this he set a kind of diminishing   reward   if the capture was effective within so many days

a thousand dollars was paid if not it was reduced gradually over a period of about a year   i

believe and   the thing was worked out very carefully because as the time elapsed between

the offer and the capture the price of the art work i believe was being reduced to keep it

equivalent   so that the whole thing operated so that the cost of the art work would be paid

to the men who apprehended the criminal by the man who bought the art work

now you say to yourself what was that what was this kind of creepy work   i mean what

was this man doing intervening was he as it were an auxiliary policeman he says "no im not an

auxiliary policeman im a sculptor"   and you say "youre a sculptor" "yes yes im making a

piece of sculpture" "why are you making a piece of sculpture?" "im making a piece of sculpture because this work doesnt mean anything   see basically this work is a solid   that is to

say it is non-committal   there is no meaning attributable to this solid object" and you say

"wait a minute solid object?" "it is as it were non-referential or non-symbolical   what it

is   is that there is an offer made by me   the work has an offer and it pays   i pay

this man a thousand dollars if he catches the criminal and i pay it with the money i receive

from my art buyer   its a perfect system   it is a sculptural system"   "say why is

that a piece of sculpture?" and it turns out to be a piece of sculpture because   and im not

putting the work down   it turns out to be a piece of sculpture because a piece of sculpture

becomes defined as a self-enclosed system referring to nothing and in doug huebler's case not

occupying physical space   hes advanced over the work that was non-committal and

occupied physical space   that is to say several years before that there was a fashion in

presenting objects which were intended as non-committal   now to say it is non-committal

that is a man fashioned oh   a cube   and the cube might be a piece of   fiberglass

and the fiberglass was placed in the room   and somebody came into the room and he

looked at the fiberglass   and then he went out having seen his piece of sculpture   now

he may not have known it was a piece of sculpture he may have thought somebody was doing something modifying the room in some manner providing it with some sort of architectural

modification but had he been a member of the sculpture relating community he would have

come to the astonishing conclusion   that an advance had taken place in sculpture   that

is to say that up to then there had been a theory of sculpture relations that went like this

sculpture consists of the coupling of elements in space   now nobody ever says that   that

is to say three-dimensional elements   arranged in three-dimensional space   people dont

say that sculpture had the idea of adding part to part   in such a manner as to energize

differentially various parts of the space   but they used to say "sculpture articulates space"

it was one of the great lines i remember everybody since about 1910 to about 1960 said

sculpture articulates space they said it about architecture too nobody knows exactly what that

meant   what it meant was   apparently   that shapes were placed in a three-dimensional

continuum and   apparently   emphasized for certain people who were remarkably sensitive

to these emphases various parts of the continuum at the expense of other parts of the continuum so

that the continuum was reduced to a non-continuum   now if that was a sculptural idea   the

idea of presenting a non-committal cube in the same three dimensional space might have been

considered by sculpture relators a move   after all you take a cube and its so big and you place it

there it also articulates space in the sense that say in this poem by wallace stevens wallace stevens talks about putting a jar in tennessee   now putting a jar in tennessee is   after all an

odd idea   merely because the scale of the jar and the scale of tennessee is discrepant

that is as soon as you say that i put a jar in tennessee   you have an idea of a relation

between a geographical entity that isnt visible and something that is trivially handleable   that

is to say you have created a kind of conceptual nexus between the jar and a state of the union

now   this peculiar activity might as it were be extended to the career of sculpture

one might say that sculpture's proceeding was to create a conceptual relation between

spaces   of a sort   now you say "what sort?" and they'd say "well   of an

interesting sort" well whats interesting about space itself?   and you could think of a lot of

things that are interesting about space but to a sculpture relator space being interesting

that is real space being interesting   lets take sculpture relators and painting relators separately

sculpture relators are interested in relations in   real space in three-dimensional space

and painting relators are involved in   in non-real space whatever they are involved in is

involved on a surface that is imagined to be separated from the space you walk into   that

is it is not typical for paintings to be placed in a doorway such that you walk through them

and that thats intrinsic to your experience   i mean people dont take a painting put it here   and you know   the gallery door is there and as you open the door you smash the

painting in half and go through thats not the way of painting   one could conceive of

somebody doing that   he would then be treating painting as a kind of entrance way

that is to say painting is an obstacle to your entry into the art gallery   when you wind up

in the art gallery you turn around and look at the hole youve made and they say that was the

painting   you know   and that may well be a way of dealing with painting   im

not   putting it down as a matter of fact there are things to be said for painting producing

that effect   but   typically painting has been regarded as living in a sacred space of its

own sacred and inviolable   that is to say it is a virtual space no matter what they do with

it   its what happens on a picture plane by itself or inside on the other side of the picture

plane   if it comes out and hits you   like in those rube goldberg cartoons you look at

it come up to it close and a little fist goes bang   then you regard it as a crypto sculpture

that is to say there was sculpture lurking in that painting you know like the man who comes

around wearing gardenias or something like that and you walk up close to him and he goes

squirt   and hits you because he had an inviolable visual object   a gardenia here

which then turned out to be a fountain   to your regret   now the point that i would

152

like to make is essentially that   painting had been imagined to be something that was

interesting in a conceptual space that was not really physical   whatever it was it wasnt really

physical   now you may say that it was perceptual and in that sense physical but the

perceptual triggered the painting and there was a career of painting and triggering activities

triggering mental activities in relation to something that as it were was marked off behind

some kind of sacred barrier   sculpture occupied a place lets say on the floor that is to say

the intrinsic thing about sculpture is that its in your world   it can fall on you you can trip

on it   it could be a terrible disaster as there was recently   dick serra killed somebody

recently   the melodrama surrounding serra's lead sculptures   that is there was always

a great deal of melodrama   largely provoked by dick and his own style   of how the

works were leaning against the wall and how they were likely to fall down and cripple people

and   if you walked along side of it you were taking your life in your hands   and there

was this feeling   that it could in fact do these things and anyone who knew anything about

leaning metal on other pieces of metal had a very bad feeling about what would finally be the

outcome but   one of them finally fell and killed someone   now he doesnt make them

that way anymore and he in fact hadnt made that one so that it should fall it had been made so that it shouldnt fall and they put it up incorrectly and   it killed someone   but the

point that im making here is that sculpture is intractably part of your space   in that sense

it even cohabits the world with you   or its an invader and   sculpture has always done

this now when you talk about painting painting has never   as it were   inhabited your

space in the same manner   now those are limiting definitions theyre not exhaustive and

they are not entirely descriptive within those areas   theres no reason why those should

be the art career   theres nothing intrinsically interesting about making painting or making

sculpture   those are merely arenas   what we have described are two arenas one arena is

in a sacred space one arena is not in a sacred space   now you say why should someone

be concerned with operating in this arena   and what sort of operation has he got in

mind in this arena   well painting as we all know has a history of presenting in some manner

beginning from an art of representation   that is to say representing some aspect of reality in

a perfectly ordinary manner that is presenting to a visual inspection some encoded message

concerning the nature of a visual reality   now thats a very cagey statement but i want to

be very cagey about it   that is i dont propose that painting was intending   to simulate

the real world at any given time   it was intending to present a representation a representation is a model   a model is not a real object and a model may always be

counted upon to   neglect certain features of the thing that it is a model of otherwise its

not a model its the thing   that is to say you make a painting of a man   there are many

features of the man that you undoubtedly leave out   if you couldnt leave out any feature

you wouldnt know that you didnt have the man   you'd have the man   now this

representational basis was not only art   it was also a function   that is to say there

were functions of representation and it is a history that painting is stuck with   sculpture

had other   things it was stuck with   there were these careers but those careers are way

in back of us   that is there are these careers so far in back of us   not because people

dont do them any more but we dont even think about them any more   because they are so

banal   that is that there were these careers of making sculpture lets say   as it were

sculpture to adorn the wall of a temple that everybody took for granted that is to say you

narrated a story in sculpture on a frieze   say   you narrated something   or you

encoded a god in an appropriate place   well thats pretty functional   and people would

know why you did it but no one would agree that that was the art function   and everybody

is aware that theres an art function and it started from some area back there and that we're here

155

making art in an arena that was not necessarily set up to be the art arena   well thats

because we're not sure what we mean when we say the art arena   we mean something

ineffably pure apparently   now what is this art arena what do we do in this art arena

and this is very curious i mean to me it seems curious because as a poet   and artist

ive always felt   secure that what i was doing was valuable to be doing   that if

someone should be doing it i should be doing it   that it needed doing   other artists

feel secure that there is something going on   and you say to yourself well what is it

that people want to do in this arena   having started with this background this absurd

background of art   which in certain cases in the case of the visual arts was a commodity at

one point it may have been sacred and at another point it was a commodity certainly from the

renaissance on art was a commodity   now i dont know how many of you people here are

artists but if all of you are artists or even a fairly large number of you are artists there are

probably very few of you who are concerned with art making as the making of a merchandisable

commodity primarily   i mean everybody figures if youre going to make art as a commodity

youre going to use that as an out   as a method to get by while you do your thing   you

know what you have in mind youre going to go to a gallery and the gallery owner is going to be

156

a jerk   and what youre going to do is youre going to convince this jerk that   what youve

got there is a sellable commodity in spite of the fact that its a piece of art   thats one attitude

another attitude is that you think the guy is really smart and you say to him you say to the

smart man nick i want you to look at this   you say nick youre a smart guy dont you think

this is very meaningful   and then you wait and if nick thinks its very meaningful it means

he thinks he can sell it to rowan then he'll think its very meaningful   but your main concern

is no matter how you feel about it you feel rather ambiguous with relation to the hustling of

merchandise   and its fairly evident   were all here and   like   there are no spies

so i think that basically we can say   that here we will feel that the selling of the thing is

secondary   that its merchandisable relations to the rest of the community   are

secondary to what we want to do   so if theyre secondary to what we want to do they may

in fact become an obstacle but they may not   the point is how do you manage with some

piece of merchandise that youve got there with something that can function as merchandise to

do something else   you want to do what   what do you want to do with this piece of

merchandise?   now think of all the kinds of merchandise that people have   people sell

old merchandise all the time   many things are merchandise for various reasons   there are people who hustle it and there are people who buy it   now think of people buying art

objects buying a painting   what does a man buy a painting for   there are a lot of buyers

there are people who buy art that is in a sense they like the art theyve seen before and presumably

they think that your work is related to it or maybe they dont maybe they consume   they

look at a work and it gives them pleasure   now you say do i really want to make a pleasure

giving machine   that is to say am i essentially in the business of trying to provide a universally

human pleasurable experience relatively durable for an average human being?   not on your

life   you know you dont think about that for a second   i mean thats ridiculous

i mean its an honourable career   but you dont think about that   that is to say the

honourable career of providing consumer value is not something that immediately occurs to you

as a matter of fact   if you think about how you go about making art   you have

a taste for things that people will find somewhat difficult   that is to say somewhat un-

comfortable   you know if they said yeah   they saw your painting and said id love to

hang it right over my sofa   youd get very nervous   you know and maybe if you got

enough money for it you wouldnt be too nervous   but on the whole you dont start out

with taking a survey to find out   if you really wanted to sell presumably youd find out what people wanted to buy   and   youd find out what it is people like   what

houses they had   how big their houses were   where you wanted to put the thing

a person has only so much wall space but you make seven by seven paintings and you

havent figured how many people have seven by seven wall space rooms   how many people

can hang a seven foot painting   have you got any idea   there are really not too many

considering the way they make houses nowadays and when you consider that they use plaster-

board rather then regular lath and plaster how do they support this thing?   you dont care

because your image is of getting it into a museum   you know perfectly well that there are

only certain places that you want that painting to go because you want it to get into a museum

which is what one might call the first stage of getting into history   that is in a certain

sense you have a very funny relation to this art work   you dont really want the man to put

it in his home   you dont care if he puts it in his home   but you hope its the kind of

man who lends paintings to traveling shows   you hope its the kind of guy who if he gives a

painting to a museum they wont throw it out the door   you know there are plenty of people

who call up museums every day in the week and say "boy have i got a painting for you"

it happens all the time   it happens all the time you know   as a matter of fact my school specializes in having an administration which is very lovable we have some of the most

lovable scientists in the country   and outside of science theyre really very astonishing people

i received a phone call from a member of the administration who said "id like you to come

over and look at a painting   to evaluate it"   and i said "why should i come look at it

to evaluate it   whats the problem?"   they said "well its being donated to the school"

i said "do we want it"   and they said "well   yes you do its—"   and they

named the name   they said its bob rhinestones painting   i said "what do you mean

its bob rhinestones painting did he paint it"   they said no   he bought it   i said

"well whose painting is it"   and they said "its a spaniard he bought it in spain"   and

i said what possessed him to buy a painting in spain? why would he go to spain to buy a

painting?   you know where did he buy it? estramadura? you know and he said to me i dont

know the name of the painter   they dont know the name of the painter they dont know

anything i should go down there and put a price tag on it   and they had a very strange idea

why should i put a price tag on it   "why youre the chairman of our art department

surely you can put the value on this painting"   and i said but i dont know anything about

estramaduran painting at this time of the year   i mean how do i know what its selling for in

160

estramadura   and the answer is   this person thought that there was an arbitrary scale

of consumer values that is fixed   that is to say   maybe not an arbitrary maybe a natural

scale of consumer values that is instantaneously apparent to us art connoisseurs   we can go

down and find the cost of a painting   we say that painting is worth two thousand three

hundred and thirty nine dollars and forty three cents and next week it will be worth   three

thousand four hundred and seventy   four cents   you know and so forth   and it

will be based on quality that is to say i will go over to that painting   and i will say yes

brush strokes fifteen hundred   color   and i will put together the components of

painting and i will lay a value on it   now while it is perfectly evident to me that this is

absurd it is not perfectly evident to the vice chancellor of the university of california   that

this   is absurd   and its for a very good reason   artists have worked very hard

to convey the illusion that   paintings are very important in a way that should carry financial

reward with them   that is usually part of our conspiracy   that when we go out into the

world   we as it were say yes thats a terrifically important painting   what do you mean

its important?   its important financially?   that is to say if it were stolen the insurance

companies would have to lay out a lot of money   everybody knows the game of insurance and paintings and what would happen finally with testimonies   a curator will be called

in and he will say yes   thats a painting of a particular sort and they pay two thousand

dollars for paintings like that   but nevertheless everybody knows perfectly well   that

a painting has no intrinsic value   that is to say monetarily its very hard to establish a

monetary value on a painting because nobody knows what anybody wants to pay for it

nobody knows what anybody wants to pay for it because nobody knows what it is theyre paying

for   now take either an old painting   old art   take old art   like a cezanne

what you have is a picture   and   what it costs is a peculiar accident undoubtedly

but the art world trys to convey an image of importance in the art activity   but they

are not willing to say what the art activity is   now   cezanne's mentality   i mean

if cezanne was working on   let us imagine that cezanne had an idea   i will not

say that he did have this idea but let me assert what cezanne's idea is   if cezanne was an

impressionist   which he was   and impressionism involved a number of people with

different attitudes but one of the most astonishing attitudes they had   was the liberation

of painting from its darkness   that is to say of opening up the possibility towards a

tremulous sunlight being rendered in paint   treating everything under a kind of trembling veil of sunlight   and that this was one of the most exciting ideas for about four

or five years   in painting   and that cezanne was one of the people who was intoxicated

with this possibility   and cezanne finally looked at it and said yes im intoxicated with sun-

light but im not intoxicated with what sunlight seems to do to volume   i mean its ridiculous

you look at what the sunlight is doing to my sense of voluminous reality   and i cant stand

it   and so he invents a style which presumably is intended to render voluminousness and

luminosity all at once   and it does it lets say   and it does this and it does this for example

at the expense of annihilating mass   cezanne's mountains always look like tablecloths

they always look like a tablecloth thats been crumpled   and theres a reason for it you

cant get everything   you know   its like gambling   art is like gambling you pay

your money you take your choice   you cant have everything at once because there are

certain things that are contradictory   in the late painting by cezanne theres no mass no

sense of mass because by the time he got through rendering volume and luminosity he has no

room for mass   that is   the characteristic that he has to sacrifice   finally

destroy the idea of weight   well thats fine   now lets say he has this idea   now he

may not have had that idea very long but there is a period during which he had that idea what is that idea worth   to a   gentleman who made himself ten million dollars in

the movie business and hes in a position to buy it   or to some gentleman who ran for office

not so long ago and didnt succeed   what is this idea worth to this man   why should

he care about cezanne's concern for improving or shifting the emphasis of an impressionist's

passion   what difference could it possibly make to him whether cezanne managed to achieve

an image of   pure configuration and luminosity   it doesnt make any difference to him

in fact it has never occurred to him that this was the idea   nor does he think the idea

is meaningful   if the idea were given to him he might say   and thats what the cezanne

is?   im turning it back in   i thought it was great art   the point is i thought this

great art was relatively eternal   you know this man was working on something   that

had a dense drive a drive that was universally clear   and was always to be found in art

but its not always to be found   is it an interesting idea?   does it interest you? i

dont know if its interesting   i mean i dont know why   i dont start from an assumption

that art has to be dealing with luminosity   now it may be that thats not interesting anymore

but it was very interesting for cezanne for a while   if cezanne lived longer it might

not have been interesting to him much afterwards   you know it might have been another

164

ten years and cezanne didnt care   now in which case if he didnt care   what if cezanne

decided he didnt care anymore about those early paintings   who cared?   his dealer?

its a very funny situation if art is about   this set of ideas that cezanne was dealing with

at the time that they were interesting   theres no inherent way of a thing holding its value

if the ideas lose their interest   now museums are there largely to capture and embalm ideas

that were once interesting   that is to place an idea that was once interesting in a place where

you can stumble over it and for reasons that are humanly valuable   reconsider the idea

that is it may be that any idea   ultimately   that is no longer available that is any

set of ideas and passions and concerns that one may call the art idea   when they disappear

may still be as valuable intrinsically as any other past idea which is gone   and that

there is something valuable about considering it from the human point of view but thats a

museum's problem   its not a problem of absolute value   it is an excercise in humanly

reevoking the world its like an exercise in shamanism   the way a shaman   evokes the

presence of the dead person   that is to say someone who is very real and had a very real

effect upon   his wife   and his children   and the tribe   and the shaman draws

upon his reality and brings him there long enough for people to recognize an anterior person who stood once fully alive   and it may very well be a terrific role that the museum

should play   it very often doesnt play it at all   and that art history should play

that is to say to play this kind of   intellectual human shamanism and i would say thats a

very respectable role but its not about value nor is it about the art youre making now   the

career that van gogh or cezanne were embarked upon seemed to them perfectly reasonable

careers   that is to say what it was that they wanted to do always seemed plausible to them

and we're in an art world   where the things that we're doing for some reason dont

immediately seem plausible   now   i dont mean by this that there is no art that is

meaningful being made in the world   that is for some reason there was a consistent series

of moves that seemed available   to people like cezanne   and so that cezanne always

knew what he wanted to do in a sense   that is he knew that there was something about

delacroix that he thought delacroix did right and there was something delacroix didnt do right

that is to say if he thought that delacroix did everything right he wouldnt have wanted to

borrow some delacroix   if he thought that he did everything wrong he wouldnt have wanted

to borrcw it either   there was a funny relation he had to delacroix   that is to say

for delacroix maybe it was right but there is something he is not doing right   now   but who is doing something for us   that is not quite right   that will clarify for us what we

should do today   i mean its a funny problem if there was a continuous career   in

which youre involved and your friend over here who just died   or who's aging is just missing

the point   of whats really important   you want to correct it for me   you know

you want to rescue whats going wrong   now what is this sense that you want to rescue?

you want to rescue a sense   something of importance   in this sense painting has

a historicity or art making has a historicity   that is to say it is a historicity of common career

he was doing something and something has gone out of the beer   its faded somewhat

something is not quite right   now i can give you an example of a situation that i feel has

faded very significantly i mean in a very realistic sense so far we have been talking in general

terms but   when   in 1965   when there appeared in new york galleries certain very

simple looking work particularly at the green gallery   certain very simple shapes thrust into

a room   and having no other justification that was obvious the shapes were placed before

you   there was something   apparently very exciting in being confronted with the idea

of simplicity   simplicity being offered to you as a significant enough object to respond to

it was in virtue of its simplicity that it accused people like disuvero of being absurd now disuvero was a very reasonable sculptor who made things by knocking things together in a

very amiable way   a tire a chain and something that hung on something else and there was

something very likable about disuvero and there was something very likable about people like

like george sugarman   who put gay little shapes together   all over the place and they

sprawled out over the floor and people liked it and they said its kind of interesting   see how

im not saying why i liked it but   people said gee it was kind of nice but on the other hand

it was kind of obvious   it was obvious in that it was a lot of movement and you said well

its a lot of movement but to no end   i mean why does he need all this machinery? why all

this coupling all this moving around?   if its possible to energize a space which people

thought was interesting to do   if its possible to energize a space   maybe its possible to

energize a space without all that obvious sign of being an art maker   maybe just one cube

in the room   what is putting a cube in a room?   or how high a cube?   that is to

say any cube?   is any cube exactly the same as any other cube?   consider the possibility

a room is a cube   make believe the room is a cube   it may not be   imagine

that the room is a cube twenty feet by twenty feet and you say to yourself the first kind of cube

that i put in that room thats going to make that room very difficult is a cube nineteen and a half feet by nineteen and a half feet by nineteen and a half feet   i assure you that that cube

is going to have a very grotesque effect and will certainly articulate the space of that room

that is if you can put that cube into the other cube   you will have articulated the space

to such a degree that almost nobody can get in there   and this is one way of articulating the

space   in this sense sculpture is an invader   that is to say sculpture then occupies space

but it calls attention to an idea   something is represented that is the possibility of art as

an invader and an aggressor and this is meaningful   now you may not want to be aggressed

upon   nevertheless in   going into an art gallery that is twenty feet by twenty feet by

twenty feet and when you encounter a cube within it that is nineteen feet by

nineteen feet by nineteen feet you still have to open the door to get in there however difficult

it may prove to be   once youre in   so that its aggression is relatively limited   you

open the door you thought there was going to be an art experience and it turns out you can

hardly get in the door   thats your first experience   on the other hand you have other

experiences which were presented earlier because that in fact was not the kind of thing that was

done   you were presented lets say with an empty room   where   a slab say three

inches off the ground and five feet wide and five feet long was presented   a square slab and

169

it was perhaps twelve inches thick   and it was three inches off the ground and you see a

few of them   lets say three of them or four of them   and you came in   thats all

there was   and   the peculiar problem is there was this large shape   it appears to

be too low   to look at head on   it appears to be   peculiarly lifted off the floor for

no purpose   that is to say you cant see under it so that its lifting off the floor is largely

obvious from   the light that falls on it   you could put your foot under it if you wanted

to   but on the whole you are apparently aware that its off the floor   yet its off-the-

floorness appears trivial because   youre damned if youre going to get on your hands and

knees and look under it   because it only has this much space under it   so a lot of

things begin to become apparent   once youre in this kind of work once you take for

granted that people will question the moves that were made   that is to say if there is a

question concerning why it is that these things were done   why it is that this thing was

three inches off the floor   and why is it that it was this size   in relation to a pre-

sentation that you would normally imagine to expect   it begins to assume a certain kind of

meaning but only if you were going to inspect it   notice that this all hinges on your

assuming some relation to a presentation in that space   up to then everybody has validated that presentation   everybody says   you come into the room and you expect to be

presented   when you come in you are presented   youre presented with something

which is different from what you intended to be presented with   and the manner in which

its different from the thing that you expected is the meaning of the work   in a sense

but notice the meaning of the work only to the degree that it is a modification of the

preceding work   that is it modifies the other work in terms of general conditions imagined

to be imposed upon presentation by the preceding history of art in   in that sense there is a

historicity there too   notice theres a live discourse   sculpture was this series of shapes

in a room   now you come in and there is only one shape and you wonder why its presentec

so low   or why its so high   or why it takes up so much room   which makes you

ask a question   is that an adequate rationale   for doing the work at all   is that

discrepancy   that discrepancy which is like a move in a chess game   is that next move

is that the meaning of the work   then you say to yourself what about the game itself

that is   thats a move in a game thats older and longer   and a game which has had

previous moves   and this is just one move   now the move has maybe changed the nature

of the overall game to some degree   but on the whole it makes you wonder about what is necessary or what is possible   and to be sure there were people in the new york art scene

who quickly saw that if you could present a cube let us say or a slab three inches off the floor

and people would in fact respond to it   that is the people who you cared about would

respond to a lot less than this   now you say what do you mean a lot less than this   this

is still merchandise   this stuff can sell   i have a set of four slabs and   somebody

comes into the gallery and says "you know i thought that was kind of terrific the way that that

operated   i have a living room thats not unlike the living room in which this was in   or

i can lower my living room or i can raise it im a serious art collector   ill raise my living

room to an auspicious size and ill put it there in the same way"   now he may very well

have found a way to house it and try the same experience   if thats what hes really interested

in   but   notwithstanding all that   how much concern is it for the artist to be able

to produce this experience again and again once its been done   that is is he producing a

reliable experience for people   to enjoy regularly   that is is he going to be happy about

the taken home work which will be there   will he bring his friends to come look at it

will he say "here is my art work?"   the logical thing is that he probably wont

that on the whole   there is a feeling that once this was done it opens up a new opportunity now theres a funny opportunity for something else   that is to make   a new theory

a new theory of what you could make with the next move and the new theory of the next

move might be that   you saw so much less in this move than in the last move   you see

that   the morris that im describing is a lot less meaningful   in any other sense than as

a modification of previous experience   well now what if we modify this in the direction of

even greater simplicity now theres no need that it should have to go in the direction of greater

simplicity but let us say   supposing that we even operate with a less   object-like thing

supposing what we do is introduce   a situation that forces questioning which this does

the slabs did force a questioning as to what they were   the first time you saw them

and   the second time perhaps   maybe for about two or three years   but by the

third year   by 1967 there was nobody terribly concerned with whether a cube was off the

ground or a slab was up in the air   it didnt matter anything like that was not only acceptable

but what you expected   now if you expected this   this isnt what the artist intended

to do   he was furthermore going to modify the situation in such a way   that you would

receive an experience   that occupied your mind for a certain length of time perhaps with

the same amount of intensity   mainly because it wasnt like this   so then let us say that you take the doug huebler as if the doug heubler were the next work   it isnt the next work

in my mind   but imagine a doug huebler piece in which doug huebler   operates

a system   he operates a system in which   he   proposes that you apprehend a

criminal and he offers the closed system   if the work is bought   if the criminal is appre-

hended the buyer pays for the apprehension   now what kind of work is that? is it a piece

of sculpture?   its an art work to the degree that is occupies your mind?   perhaps

its not an object and its a piece of sculpture to huebler   now huebler sees it   hes

chipped away a certain amount of the physical materiality of sculpture   and yet retained

the kind of displacement character of minimal art   that is   the work is entirely displaced

spatially   i mean forgetting all the other aspects of it the sociological and humanitarian

about which one might raise some very interesting questions   but there is a displace-

ment   the work itself involves   history and geography   there is someone who has

been identified by documentation as a committer of a crime somewhere in the past   what-

ever crime   and his name is known and a photograph is given of him   in order to capture

him somebody would have to go out and find   such a person to   conform essentially

to the photograph   and to the history   that is ultimately someone who conforms to

174

the photograph will be supposed to conform to the history and then   other tests will be

invoked to find out whether the person conforms to the name as well as the history   now

that will be done   and then   this particular situation will invoke a necessary reward or

initial outlay of money by huebler   say a thousand dollars that huebler will have to put

up because the art work hasnt been sold yet   and then this whole thing will be sold   as

an art work   this is a   comical idea   you notice the comedy   now you say to

yourself "but huebler that's not physical space"   and huebler says "no but its real space"

its very real space   police action only occurs in real space   sculpture occurs in

real space   its a sculpture   sculpture is real space this is real space   real space is

experience space   its not physical space   its not three-dimensional twenty by twenty

space   its not the space of this room   as a   three-dimensional manifold that is

metrically determined   thats not human space   human space is experiential

space   i dont experience the part of the room that those six people are sitting on though

it is metrically possible   i could refer it to axes that are arbitrarily there   but thats

not a space i recognize   i may recognize the people   i may move from part to part

with my mind   but   not all of this room   is experienced humanly by me at any given time   and i only refer to the room as a conceptual continuum   i think thats

fairly obvious to everybody   its almost banal on the other hand human space is   a

kind of   conceptual manifold that is   not continuous   its the space of experience

that is the space of all kinds of experience   tactile   social   literary

acoustical olfactory   i mean its a very complicated operation   huebler presents a piece

that operates   or could conceivably operate in real space   there is a danger of it

becoming real space   now there is the danger of it occupying moral space   if you

picked out   i think that with deliberate malice huebler picked out a criminal whose

criminality first of all is neither clear nor significant   that is he happened to wind up on a

wanted list despite   the fact that   his crime seemed to be publically real and though he

may not have committed the crime he looked marvelously innocent   that is the photograph

of a man who looks terrifically unlikely as a criminal   and what youre being invited to do

is participate   in what one might call a potential obscenity   that is to say youre being

invited to take part in the apprehension of the human being only on the faith   that the

wanted poster is accurate   this raises the question about the accuracy of the documentation

of the first part and it offers this problem as a temptation   it offers the art work as a temptation to crime of its own sort so that it evokes this moral space   a very curious moral

space is evoked by this work   now you say this art work is an interesting art work for a

very good reason   its not an interesting art work because its a work modifying art history

its an interesting art work because it raises the question about the meaning of art   it

raises the question about what sort of space a work of art could possibly occupy   and huebler

is in a certain sense paradoxically suggesting   what about occupying this insane moral space

i mean consider it   huebler always presents it as if it were a formalist scheme

everything is beautifully presented   that is   you capture the man youre paid the

thousand dollars   huebler receives a thousand dollars from the buyer of the art work

the buyer of the art work is thereby the man who finances the whole operation and there is

neither gain nor loss   as a matter of fact huebler is not profiting   the piece was aimed

at non-profit   its a non-profit art work now take the structural piece which is very curious

and regard it as formalist sculpture   the work itself from the historical and abstract art

point of view is very ironic   what the work does is create a kind of total irony   with

respect to formalist concerns in sculpture   it raises the idea that formal concerns applied

to things that might be interesting   in human space   would turn out to be obscene on the other hand that's very interesting   it raises the issue essentially of what i

would call pornography   now art has always played with pornography in the west   i

mean pornography has been a very significant concern of art in the west   its been significant

because it has always been the challenge   of the artist that art is informal because one

responds pornographically   the most cheerful aspect   the most heartening aspect about

western european art was its possible pornographic concerns   because it was always the

spectre of the human   however formal an art work was if it played with pornography as an

idea   not because the pornography was beautiful or cheerful   but because   it was

a reminiscence of human manuever within the work   now   if hueblers work   is

an assault on it   there are many works in the art world that are not   i picked hueblers

work because hueblers work is an art work of a rather odd kind   he presents it as a formalist

non-representational piece and what it is is a rather bizarre model of reality   that is it is a

representational piece of sculpture   if it is sculpture it is representational sculpture

but there are many   sculptural works that are not   consider   take a dennis oppenheim

work   dennis oppenheim did a piece of work in which he managed to get some things harvested

in a field i dont remember if it was wheat or corn or what it was but he harvested it   he

178

harvested it   he arranged the field in such a manner as to correspond to the route between

there and the place he was shipping the   grain to   he harvested the grain by making

this contour pattern in the area and when he harvested the grain he sent it to an art gallery

and   the grain was sold   now big deal   i mean thats   formal   there was

a task   an arbitrary relation between field and grain   which was there   and the

natural environment and the removal   of the grain into an art context where it became

a commodity   that is it was labeled art and it was sold   now   theoretically

the works look like they have the same structural   center   that is to say they

work in human space   the oppenheim harvests   corn or wheat and it goes through a

situation in which the activity   the costly labor of oppenheim and the people are then paid

for by the purchase of a patron say   say rowan   whats the difference theyre paid for

by   the pasadena museum's large backer and   you know he buys the grain   he

wont because it doesnt look like an olitsky   but thats not the point   the fact is

he pays for it and that makes it a complete cycle   its a perfect system   now you say

to yourself they did a perfect system of the same order as the huebler   i mean is it

interesting the way the huebler is interesting   the huebler verges on obscenity and triviality

179

and   the huebler is a very violent piece   thats why huebler is one of the best of the

conceptual artists and there are very few good conceptual artists   i mean that is why

huebler is a profoundly disturbing artist and oppenheims not disturbing theres nothing disturbing

about an oppenheim piece   not of that type   now   consider   other kinds

of work   now i dont remember if it was oppenheim or heizer who did this piece   and

there is a very interesting and very violent conceptual work   that is done by one of them

which was   the   police dog piece that was done in boston   its a different kind of

piece than the huebler piece   the huebler piece verges on social structures and sociology

in a way what im talking about is a social art that doesnt work within an arbitrary formalist

frame but this piece which was either oppenheims or heizers   and if i dont remember which

one it is its because i begin to think of them as the bobbsey twins at times   involved the

placement of police dogs in front of the museum near the entrance to the museum and these

police dogs were chained   they were   chained down in such a way that if you walked

a straight line between them the police dogs however violent they got   would not be able

to reach you   but they would come very close   now i would say that articulated the

space rather clearly   the space was articulated very well   you walked down the space the animals lunged at you   and you found that the space was very narrow   there

were three inches on either side which were not dog   and you got into the museum

to get into the museum you had to go by these rather   peculiar animals   now

theres something interesting about that and amusing   a kind of witty idea   but now

this dog work occupies a space somewhere between the oppenheim cancelled crop operation

and the huebler piece   the violent relation this sort of funny special path to the

museum   now you think about the piece itself as a model of art structure   that is the

art structure being represented as a model path into a museum   it is an amusing idea and

kind of   terrifying in a funny way   theres something interesting and peculiar about

its operation   its trivial in a sense that you know the animals are not going to kill you

its trivial   oh   you may not believe in the secure technological   assurance

of those chains   one knows of those mistakes made by industry before   i mean one

knows that lockheed exists   if lockheed exists its possible that the chains may not exist

all the time   lockheed has planes that dont exist very well   i mean why should the

chains hold up all the time   still youre toying with fear in a more or less pornographic

sense   i mean this kind of work shares a pornographic character   with the huebler what youre offered is a kind of *frisson* a kind of chilling quality in the work and youre

setting up the chilling quality by trying out the art work   in a way   this piece

questions art making too in relation to pornography   that is it questions it because the art

itself   handles human feelings   toys with human feelings in a situation   that is

ultimately rather protected which is pornography and it is self provoking   you enter into

it   now apparently   to the degree that   both pieces are rather melodramatic

i dont mean to advocate only melodramatic operation   but youll notice that both of

these operations are about pornography in art   they are about art as it were opportunizing

over social   human activities   now it seems one of the problems here thats raised is

the kind of conflict that exists between human values and the idea of art making itself as a career

that is   what art making is about   or what it has often been about   take the

nude say   the female nude   from the renaissance on it has always offered something

of an entrance to the painting through human sexual feeling   the consumer   the art

looker   was always assumed to be a man   now everyone knows that men dont get

excited when they see a painting of a beautiful naked woman   not a gentleman or an art

lover   relator   not now anyway that we have photographs and movies   still who can deny that there is that momentary flicker of interest   sure its more complicated than

that   this feeling is surely diverted or suspended   by some conflict of interest

in painting say or antiquity   nostalgia   still its a naked woman youre looking at in a

titian or a renoir   or a wesselman   it isnt a wine bottle or a mountain   though

the feeling   the flicker   of sexuality is protected from its consequences by its surrounding

attributes   its props   the case is   may be clearer with suffering than with sexuality

the painter has painted a picture of a human being in torment   you are filled with an

honorable   ennobling sympathy for his exquisite torment   you look at gruenewald's

christ and are filled with pleasure   youre masturbating at the crucifixion   we are back

to vito acconci   what is the point of all this self stimulation if you are the viewer   or

why all this generosity if you are the artist   this sexual assistance?   what are you masters

and johnson?   at least for vito the pleasure is reciprocal   he sits under a plank conceal-

ment and knows that you   the audience   are only a few feet away from his trivial but

scandalous pleasure   he knows that you are nearby and he is pleased to be so close to dis-

closure his *frisson* you are close to his sexual act about as close as you are to it any time you

walk by the door of somebody else's apartment   but you know that your being there gives him pleasure and   his being there   gives you pleasure   this is a little fairer

then pornography as it is usually practiced in the arts   but what if you are not especially

interested in or in need of masturbation   for an artist who gets no *frisson* from exposing

himself   or pretending to do so what is there to do?   supposing art making is like a

kind of knot making   if youre a knot maker youve got an idea about what is a knot and

what is a mess   a legal way of proceeding   what is a legal knot and what is a snarl?

all knots involve some kind of double reversal   you start out   going somewhere go back

and take some of the past with you   to wherever you were going to go and you find a way

to mark off some memorial to where youve been   a node   well there are two kinds at

least   of knot makers   one knot maker knows how to proceed making his knots and

watches himself proceding   in the end he arrives at a knot he approves   for some

reason   if he's been watching the way he has been knotting all this time he wont be

surprised at the outcome   and though he may be satisfied he will walk away and forget it

then he's a process knot maker   or he might not walk away but place it in front of

you in the hope that you will be bettered thereby   in which case he's a therapeutic   or

didactic knot maker   or say he is a forgetful knot maker   as soon as he finishes a loop he forgets it   because all the time he is only attending to the node he is working on at any

given moment   at some time when he's tired or interrupted by a phone call he will look up

and he'll be surprised by his knot because he'll have no idea how he got there   he's a kind

of magical knot maker   but with all of this   and i think we should   not under-

estimate the pleasures and surprises of knot making   why in the world should we bother

making knots who cares about rope?   in a way this is a lot like playing chess and you can

say someone has played it well or played poorly but   why should you care about this game?

it seems ridiculous to spend all this time pushing little pieces of wood about on a board

havent you got better things to do?   but it was not always this way with chess

chess is a depraved game   it represents the world as a struggle for dominance between two

sides that have no choice but conflict   there is no clear demarcation or boundary that cuts

off one side from the others hostilities   and there is no bound to human abilities   it is

an arrogant fantasy of war   in which the greater ability will surely win   by annihilating

his opponent   what sort of paradigm is this?   no experience on earth corresponds to

it   so it is a game of no relevance   it is a fundamentally trivial representation of reality

but it wasnt always like that   according to most authorities chess derived from an

185

indian game called *shatrandji*   which was supposed to represent the state of the world

the social classes into which people were arbitrarily divided   and it was a game invaded by

chance   the best player   the best plan   could as easily be defeated as the worst

by luck   and this was thought to teach humility to rulers   *shatrandji* was the

game of which chess is the trivial example   and it doesnt seem that we have to be especially

impressed with *shatrandji* either   but as *shatrandji* was a game built up out of the human

experiences of its time   arbitrary inequities among people   the facts of unavoidable

war   and the absurd circumstances of luck lying under the feet of ability   it is possible

to construct   make our art out of something more meaningful than the arbitrary rules of

knot making   out of the character of human experience in our world

Looking Back at *Talking*

Nineteen seventy-one is a long time ago, longer ago than the First World War seemed to us when we were little kids on the eve of the Second. We knew that back then the aces of the Lafayette Escadrille flew little biplanes and people looked funny in the straw hats and seersucker suits they wore in summer, but it was only twenty-three years from 1941 back to 1918, and it's thirty years back to 1971. Yet 1971 in America won't go away, the way the Vietnam War won't go away, at least for me. We were living— my wife Elly and my three-year-old son Blaise and I—in a crumbly old stucco house perched on a bluff right over the ocean in a sleepy little coastal town north of San Diego called Solana Beach. From the back terrace you could watch the surfers and look flying seagulls in the eye. We were recent transplants from New York City and we'd lived most of our lives in the intense metropolitan world of Manhattan, where everything was always happening and everybody was always arguing about it. And now we lived in Solana Beach, where nothing was happening, or nothing you could really see.

Sure, our baby-sitter's boyish mother, the graphic designer who lived across the street with her husband and two kids, was drinking too much and slowly getting ready to leave her husband for a girlfriend who was a biologist at Scripps. But it took her five years to do it. Mrs. Harris, the elderly widow who lived in the beautifully overgrown house up the street, was finding it harder and harder to walk back from the Mayfair market at the bottom of the hill. The lady with the elegant Swedish husband and Afghan was starting a lunch-hour affair with the good-looking, older lifeguard who ran the station at our local beach. Mr. Canton, the retired actuary, was feeling poorly and thinking of going to live with his brother in Montreal. And the husband of the retired teacher who scolded us for letting weeds grow on our front lawn sat resolutely in his open garage playing cocktail piano and glaring at anyone who passed by. And all the while the war was going on and long-haired teenage boys disappeared one by one into the navy or the marines, though the only way you could tell was by walking down the hill to check out the headlines in the newspaper dispenser in front of the post office or the local market.

I got fascinated with these glass-faced newspaper dispensers whose bold headlines spilled disasters from Europe and Asia or Africa undetected through the glass panels into the sunny streets in front of the quiet little markets, the sleepy auto repair shops and local bank branches, libraries and drugstores. So without thinking too much about it, I started photographing them. But every day for about thirty days I went to another place, taking care to shoot the newspaper in such a way that you could read the headline and still see the dispenser situated in its untroubled San Diego neighborhood. It was about this time that Lita Hornick asked me if I had a book I wanted to do for her new poetry series.

So *Talking* was a book that came together rather suddenly. It was late in 1971. Lita was the publisher of *Kulchur,* an art and literary magazine for which I'd written a couple of Art Chronicles, and she was starting to publish books. *Meditations,* my last book, had finally come out earlier that year. It had been composed in 1969 and I was irritated because John Martin had taken so long to publish it. So I was glad to get away from Black Sparrow, and nobody seemed to understand the book anyway. I was determined that any new book was going to be very different. I started putting it together, and for the most part it was. The poems of *Meditations,* like *Code of Flag Behavior* and *definitions,* looked like poems. They were a procedural poetry that drew on source texts subjected to various operations and organized in verse lines. None of the works in *Talking* looked like poems. Because I didn't want them to. I was sick of the look of poems— my poems and everybody else's. So "The November Exercises" looked like some kind of journal. "Three Musics for Two Voices" and "The London March" were laid out like musical scores, and "Talking at Pomona" looked like an eccentrically notated talk, which it was. And the book led off with the one-liner:

> if someone came up and started talking a poem at you
>
> how would you know it was a poem?

"The November Exercises" was just what it claimed to be—a series of exercises undertaken several times a day—the time markings tell how many. It was November 1971 and I was in a down mood. So they functioned as a kind of a cross between calisthenics and spiritual exercises, operating on the events of the daily news or my personal life by means of a handbook for foreigners, *Essential Idioms of English.* I started on November 1st and ran out of steam by November 27th.

"Three Musics for Two Voices" started earlier—back in 1968. When I left the Institute of Contemporary Art in Boston, where I was Educational Curator in 1967, to come out to San Diego, Sue Thurman, who was the director then, asked me to think about making an audiotape for visitors to the Institute. Since the ICA was a *kunsthalle,* not a museum, and had no permanent collection, I had a fairly free hand. I thought of designing a piece to raise the question of how to come to terms with something new and unknown without turning it into another example of what you already knew. I'm not sure if anything I worked on would have been useful to the Institute's visitors, but I never found out. The ICA ran out of money, Sue lost her job, and I was free to do whatever I wanted to do with the piece. As it happened, Dan Graham called me right about then. He was editing an "Information Theory" issue of *Aspen* magazine and wanted to know if I would contribute something. I thought I would take up the project I'd started thinking about for the ICA. I had an old experimental design book left over from my college days and decided to use it as the basis of a controlled improvisation that I asked my wife Elly to help me with. Elly, though a conceptual artist, was an experienced actress and good at improvising. I typed out the text that I wanted her to read and that I was going to question, and set it up so she could either respond to my questions or continue reading. We turned on a tape recorder and tried it. We'd listen to the recordings and when I didn't like a take, we'd try it again. In half a dozen takes we got the whole thing.

"The London March" was different. I set it up as a kind of radio play. Elly had the habit of playing solitaire for various whimsical wishes, and we'd learned that there was a pathetic little anti-Vietnam War march being organized by Americans in London. We were in San Diego, so that was the other side of the world as far as we were concerned, and the Vietnam war wasn't an English war, it was an American war. I got the idea that Elly should play for the success of the march, whatever that might mean, while we listened to KNX, an all news radio station, trying to find out what if anything was happening in London. I typed out a loose scenario. Late that night I turned on the radio, and Elly and I improvised the rest in a single take. The spliced together version of "Three Musics for Two Voices" and the single take of "The London March," poorly recorded in our kitchen, were played in a "reading" at St. Mark's in the Bowery in December 1968. Dan Graham published the final text of "Three Musics for Two Voices" in an issue of *Aspen* Magazine in a crazed Fluxus format designed by my friend George Maciunas as a separate pamphlet with pages six inches wide and one and a half inches high. My photographs turned into a photo piece I referred to as "30 Days of the News." I never showed it anywhere, but I cut up the strips of contact prints, assembled them in rows and used them as the inside and outside covers of the original edition of *Talking*.

DAVID ANTIN

2001

LANNAN SELECTIONS

The Lannan Foundation, located in Santa Fe, New Mexico, is a family foundation whose funding focuses on special cultural projects and ideas which promote and protect cultural freedom, diversity, and creativity.

The literary aspect of Lannan's cultural program supports the creation and presentation of exceptional English-language literature and develops a wider audience for poetry, fiction, and nonfiction.

Since 1990, the Lannan Foundation has supported Dalkey Archive Press projects in a variety of ways, including monetary support for authors, audience development programs, and direct funding for the publication of the Press's books.

In the year 2000, Lannan Selections was established to promote both organizations' commitment to the highest expressions of literary creativity. The foundation supports the publication of this series of books each year, and works closely with the Press to ensure that these books will reach as many readers as possible and achieve a permanent place in literature. Authors whose works have been published as Lannan Selections include: Ishmael Reed, Stanley Elkin, Ann Quin, Nicholas Mosley, William Eastlake, and David Antin, among others.

◫
DALKEY ARCHIVE PAPERBACKS

PIERRE ALBERT-BIROT, *Grabinoulor.*
YUZ ALESHKOVSKY, *Kangaroo.*
FELIPE ALFAU, *Chromos.*
   Locos.
   Sentimental Songs.
ALAN ANSEN,
   Contact Highs: Selected Poems 1957-1987.
DAVID ANTIN, *Talking.*
DJUNA BARNES, *Ladies Almanack.*
   Ryder.
JOHN BARTH, *LETTERS.*
   Sabbatical.
AUGUSTO ROA BASTOS, *I the Supreme.*
ANDREI BITOV, *Pushkin House.*
ROGER BOYLAN, *Killoyle.*
CHRISTINE BROOKE-ROSE, *Amalgamemnon.*
GERALD L. BRUNS,
   Modern Poetry and the Idea of Language.
GERALD BURNS, *Shorter Poems.*
GABRIELLE BURTON, *Heartbreak Hotel.*
MICHEL BUTOR,
   Portrait of the Artist as a Young Ape.
JULIETA CAMPOS,
   The Fear of Losing Eurydice.
ANNE CARSON, *Eros the Bittersweet.*
CAMILO JOSÉ CELA, *The Hive.*
LOUIS-FERDINAND CÉLINE, *Castle to Castle.*
   London Bridge.
   North.
   Rigadoon.
HUGO CHARTERIS, *The Tide Is Right.*
JEROME CHARYN, *The Tar Baby.*
MARC CHOLODENKO, *Mordechai Schamz.*
EMILY HOLMES COLEMAN,
   The Shutter of Snow.
ROBERT COOVER, *A Night at the Movies.*
STANLEY CRAWFORD,
   Some Instructions to My Wife.
RENÉ CREVEL, *Putting My Foot in It.*
RALPH CUSACK, *Cadenza.*
SUSAN DAITCH, *Storytown.*
PETER DIMOCK,
   A Short Rhetoric for Leaving the Family.
COLEMAN DOWELL, *The Houses of Children.*
   Island People.
   Too Much Flesh and Jabez.
RIKKI DUCORNET, *The Complete Butcher's Tales.*
   The Fountains of Neptune.
   The Jade Cabinet.
   Phosphor in Dreamland.
   The Stain.
WILLIAM EASTLAKE, *The Bamboo Bed.*
   Castle Keep.
   Lyric of the Circle Heart.

STANLEY ELKIN, *Boswell: A Modern Comedy.*
   Criers and Kibitzers, Kibitzers and Criers.
   The Dick Gibson Show.
   The MacGuffin.
   The Magic Kingdom.
   The Rabbi of Lud.
ANNIE ERNAUX, *Cleaned Out.*
LAUREN FAIRBANKS, *Muzzle Thyself.*
   Sister Carrie.
LESLIE A. FIEDLER,
   Love and Death in the American Novel.
FORD MADOX FORD, *The March of Literature.*
JANICE GALLOWAY, *Foreign Parts.*
   The Trick Is to Keep Breathing.
WILLIAM H. GASS, *The Tunnel.*
   Willie Masters' Lonesome Wife.
ETIENNE GILSON, *The Arts of the Beautiful.*
   Forms and Substances in the Arts.
C. S. GISCOMBE, *Giscome Road.*
   Here.
KAREN ELIZABETH GORDON, *The Red Shoes.*
PATRICK GRAINVILLE, *The Cave of Heaven.*
HENRY GREEN, *Blindness.*
   Concluding.
   Doting.
   Nothing.
JIŘÍ GRUŠA, *The Questionnaire.*
JOHN HAWKES, *Whistlejacket.*
ALDOUS HUXLEY, *Antic Hay.*
   Point Counter Point.
   Those Barren Leaves.
   Time Must Have a Stop.
GERT JONKE, *Geometric Regional Novel.*
DANILO KIŠ, *A Tomb for Boris Davidovich.*
TADEUSZ KONWICKI, *A Minor Apocalypse.*
   The Polish Complex.
ELAINE KRAF, *The Princess of 72nd Street.*
EWA KURYLUK, *Century 21.*
DEBORAH LEVY, *Billy and Girl.*
JOSÉ LEZAMA LIMA, *Paradiso.*
OSMAN LINS, *The Queen of the Prisons of Greece.*
ALF MAC LOCHLAINN,
   The Corpus in the Library.
   Out of Focus.
D. KEITH MANO, *Take Five.*
BEN MARCUS, *The Age of Wire and String.*
WALLACE MARKFIELD, *Teitlebaum's Window.*
   To an Early Grave.
DAVID MARKSON, *Collected Poems.*
   Reader's Block.
   Springer's Progress.
   Wittgenstein's Mistress.
CARL R. MARTIN, *Genii Over Salzburg.*
CAROLE MASO, *AVA.*

Visit our website: www.dalkeyarchive.com

DALKEY ARCHIVE PAPERBACKS

Visit our website: www.dalkeyarchive.com